"Challenged... If you are looking for a book to challenge you to pick up your cross and follow Jesus, this is your book! I was encouraged through the pages of this book, even when life crumbles and falls apart the Lord ultimately has a purpose. Derek Diaz's testimony is an inspiring one of how Jesus can mend the deepest wounds, restore identity, and release us into abundant freedom. He shared the gospel in such a practical way. Helping to put into perspective for all who are looking to know Jesus, not in theory, but rather through a personal and transformative relationship. Why Did I Get Saved? helps believers understand the fundamental question, have I encountered Jesus personally? If so, was I transformed by who I encountered?"
- *Karina Nardi*
Biblical Counselor Makarios International Puerto Plata, Dominican Republic

"From the very first words that Derek begins this book with, it's very clear what jumps out from his heart--love and reconciliation. Derek illustrates so clearly what many Christians view of Christianity may be: you should be focused more on what you think you should do, as opposed to who you are. As he details his life's story, the celebrations, the triumphs, the betrayals, and the valleys, it becomes evident that his passion for the body of Christ burns deeply, burns to see people change, and burns for people to really experience the transformative power of Jesus. Even in the midst of things mentioned in this book, one thing is certain, Jesus is real. It is my belief that everyone whose eyes glance at the pages of this book will feel the love and desire Christ has for them. That they will be forever changed, just as he was in that Christmas Eve service."
- *Dr. Timothy Bradford Jr.*
Associate Pastor - The Bridge, Columbus, MS

"In the modern era of Christian personal memoirs, such narratives often focus on the internal turmoil of sin causing poor choices and exhaustive emotional vulnerability. Expressing vulnerability is healthy and authentic in Christian literature and explorative texts, however without the articulation of the Person of Christ within the story the reader cannot comprehend the greater narrative or connection to the Gospel message. Derek successfully bridges the gap between his own personal struggle with loss, betrayal, pride, and anguish with the present redemption of Jesus within his own story which expresses God's desire to "work all things for good for those who love Him and are called by His purpose." Reading the pages of this book will not only allow you to become intimately acquainted with Derek but the Person of Christ. Sound theology, relatable story-telling, relevant modern contexts, and attention-grabbing scenarios will help the reader to reconcile their own struggles in the discovery of the ever-present Jesus amidst Derek's narrative and their own life. I wholeheartedly recommend Derek's recent book and his ministry as I believe him to be genuine, a transparent & accurate voice to the Church, and a true disciple of Jesus Christ."

-Daniel Gurry
Founder, 4 Corners International

"A heart of a true evangelist and that's who Derek Daniel Diaz is. In this book, you will learn that he is genuine and real as he goes on this journey in seeking and anchoring himself in Jesus. Jeremiah 29:13 says "If you look for me wholeheartedly, you will find me." You will not stay passive after reading this book. It will steer up real emotions in you and invite you to ask questions, process your pain, and push you forward to search deeper for God than before."

- Mufa David Besic, M. Div.
Pastor at Upper Room Dallas

"I've known and walked alongside Derek Diaz for the last few years and I can attest to the power and reality of what God has done in his life. His book, *"Why Did I Get Saved?"* is his testimony of how God took this young man, and saved, delivered and healed him. Derek carries the friendship of God on his life and his story will awaken you to walk in a closer and more intimate way with God. I love Derek and I love this book."
- *Corey Russell*
Author and Pastor at Upper Room Church

The written word brings about a response from the reader; one that is private, personal, authentic. Some authors seek to expand our imagination, some seek empathy, or a response from the reader in the public square. Derek Diaz through his written story seeks to draw love out of the hearts of his readers. He seeks a response, but not a response to him or anyone else; he seeks a response to Jesus. He wants anyone who reads his story to fall more in love with Jesus. Regardless of the response the reader may have to the content, the theology, the worldview, etc., one cannot ignore the clear call to Christ that Derek shouts. I exhort you to see the strong character that is within Derek. Not only is he a selfless man of God, but he is a man full of love for his fellow man. He seeks the best for anyone that comes into contact with his story. May you be healed by it as he was healed.
- *Grant Waldron*
Graduate Student, Dallas Theological Seminary

DEREK D. DIAZ

Why Did I Get Saved?

How Christianity Failed Me But Jesus Filled Me

PUBLISHING

I dedicate this book to John Chau. You still are an inspiration and will forever be one in my life. Thank you for living out the commandment Jesus spoke over in John 15: 12-13. No greater love than one who would lay down his life for his friends. John I never met you but I can still feel your heart and love for Jesus and it burns so deeply inside me now. Thank you for giving your life to the Gospel and I pray the flame of your story never burns out. Thank you John.

"May these pages take me places my tongue can't…"

DEREK D. DIAZ

Contents

Foreword

In 1897, Andrew Murray wrote, in *The Ministry of Intercession*, that *"Every child of God has the Holy Spirit in him to pray. God waits to give the Spirit in full measure. Our Lord gave the Holy Spirit to His disciples on His resurrection day to enable them to wait for the full outpouring on the day of Pentecost. It is only in the power of the Spirit already in us, acknowledged and yielded to, that we can pray for His fuller manifestation."*

How incredibly compassionate is the Father that allows His children to wait for the outpouring of the fullness of the Holy Spirit. He knows that our ways are not His ways, that our thoughts are not His thoughts. We have all of the Spirit that we are going to get and yet the manifestation of the fullness of power is dependent upon the yielded position of the heart, and that my friend can take a while.

My wife, Ruth, had heard of a new church being launched in our hometown in South Florida in 2018. We began regularly attending if the doors were open, we were there. The congregation was overwhelmingly made up of Gen Z and Millennials who for the most part had come from mega-churches in the area. I had truly thought that in America, we had lost these generations, that in staggering numbers Gen Z and Millennials had either left the church or were totally unchurched. What a joy to find a sincere love of Christ, an authentic interest in community, and a level of transparency in their walk that, quite frankly, I never experienced in my generation. The church was alive with hope and energy and Ruth and I threw ourselves into walking alongside our new family. We were 30 years older than most of the congregation and while that felt occasionally odd it was also uplifting as we poured ourselves out. It was in this context that Ruth and I had the honor of ministering in a lay capacity with Derek.

His story is, if you have been saved for more than a few years, is like most Christian walks: Exuberant in our salvation, consumed by the palpable love of Christ, hungry for all that is God, and eager to get to work. Then we are faced with walking out life. Setbacks happen, offenses come, and we are bombarded with a world system that is at its core is evil. Walking out our salvation without the fullness of the power of the Holy Spirit is a fool's game.

But I am reminded in Paul's letter to the Philippian church:

"Therefore, my beloved, as you have always obeyed, not as in my presence only, but now much more in my absence, work out your own salvation with fear and trembling; for it is God who works in you both to will and to do for His good pleasure. Do all things without complaining and disputing, that you may become blameless and harmless, children of God without fault in the midst of a crooked and perverse generation, among whom you shine as lights in the world," Philippians 2:12-15 NKJV.

I have watched Derek navigate his salvation by responding rightly to adversity, completely surrendering to the centrality of Jesus Christ, and through yielding his heart in prayer receive the fullness of the Holy Ghost. In this crucial hour, I pray that all of us will listen to this message that God has placed in Derek's heart.

-Tom Mansmith

Acknowledgement

Thank you first to the team of people in West Palm Beach, FL that first walked me through the season of my life with much grace and mercy.

Thank you to the Mansmith's for fathering and mothering me through a difficult time in my life. I pray that all those hours spent on that floor and carpet will reap a harvest 100x fold.

A special thanks to Tom Mansmith for giving me guidance on how this book would be written.

Thank you to Karina Nardi for putting up with me and my stubbornness as I grew in the Lord to get to this place to finish the book. You inspired me to never give up and spoke to the man God showed you not the man you saw.

Thank you to Martha Serrano, your initial editorial process and comments on the book fueled the book to become more than just a story.

Thank you to Roy Kamau and your organization, GREAT Books, for the united collaboration and effort in the process of writing this book and seeing it to completion. Your faithfulness and gentleness in your leadership are truly a gift to the body.

Thank you to Diana for this wonderful cover and how it beautifully portrays God's vision for the moment in my life. I bless you all greatly and you are all priceless.

Introduction

"Why did I get saved"? The title might throw you off. The question reads this way, what was the point of my salvation. I started writing this book from a stage in my life where I didn't have any answers. Sadly, I didn't have them because I didn't spend time asking God why. I started writing this at the desk of my old job, hoping it would be my last workplace.

I am also writing this book at what I could consider the lowest point of my life, that rock bottom moment. It's why this book is not a story about my actual salvation; it's about my journey of giving my life to Christ and coming to the place of asking myself, what was the point?

To fully understand where I am coming from, I'm excited to unravel my story from the time I first encountered Jesus, to the place I had to make a real decision to stay with Him. I promise it won't be an autobiography as I'm not that important, but understanding my background will help you know why I wrote this book.

What is my hope in you reading this book? It is to give you the truest faith-based Jesus encounter testimony. This story is not like yours or other people's testimony. Our differences are the reason why most testimonies are so exciting.

My story is not a story about a long life of running away and having this amazing transformative encounter and "Boom!" my life changes. This is a story about what to do when you've already given your all to Him, but the devil knocks the wind out of you while pulling the rug from beneath you.

As I wrote this, I was honestly questioning my faith - you'll understand why later. I'm still a follower of Jesus, but I doubted a lot of Christianity, not necessarily God, just Christianity. My heart and my mind were not in the right place, which is why this book is almost two years in the making. Yet, I want to be clear that this is not a book to blame God or the church or people, although I did choose to include them in the mess. This way, as humans, we can work on being better together.

You might find this book to be somewhat critical, and I'm glad if you do. We have spent too much time not addressing the bride (Christian Church) and not calling her up to the position she was meant to stand at. My criticism is not because I'm upset with the church. It's because I love the church, and I love its people so much, and I am truly grieved to know both the church and the world see God from a tainted place.

We must face reality and realize we are much to blame for why people are running away from Christians and the church. We have sold them a cheap gospel that doesn't require any investment on their part. We have promised them big dreams and good lives as long as they do two things, serve the church and tithe their money. My heart burns to see sold-out people fill the church, not because they *need* the church but because they are content and satisfied with God. Not leaning on man, but knowing that God is always with them.

I believe that by the end of this book, a big decision will come across your plate. I hope that a question will stir up some action in you to pursue something greater than your wellbeing and that this piece of my life places you in a position to hear from God as I did, maybe from an unconventional place.

This book reminds me of the story of Job in the Bible. So many people love that book because of Job's faithfulness toward God and God's faithfulness at the very end toward Job amid really harsh trials. The reality of Job's life was the entire book was not his whole life but just a snip of it. Whether you find yourself in the beginning, the middle, or the end (figuratively), I can promise one thing God is with you and can turn all things around for His glory.

Trust me, I'm really eccentric, and you'll probably enjoy the way I tell this story. One thing this book is not - it is not an answer. After all, Jesus is the answer. Seeking Him and not a story of Him always gives you the perfect peace you need to move forward in any situation you find yourself in.

Jesus is the Light unto our path. With this book, I am providing a path to the Light, not a light to the path.

My story is exactly that—my story. In no way do I support anyone saying, "Oh, because it happened to Derek, it can happen for me this way too." Wrong! I repeat this is not a "get out of my problems book." This is not a "read this book to answer your very specific issues and use this to solve them." Jesus is the Light unto our path.

With this book, I am providing a path to the Light, not a light to the path. May this book make you laugh, cry, hope, wonder, and believe that God has a perfect plan for you. He knows the exact plans for your life no matter how "lost" or "found" you may believe you are; you can rest knowing He has the final say. Allow Him to write your story as He did mine. So that you will not have to find yourself one day asking, "Why Did I Get Saved?" as I did.

* * *

The Confusion
I sit back and see all those around me who have what I don't and live how I wish
How can they achieve when I continue to fail?
What I am doing wrong, why can't I prevail?
Even with money in the bank, girls on my side, I still feel empty, dead on the inside
I have no life, yet people strive to be like me
They slave over jobs and spend when they don't just to taste and see
I'm sitting in luxury
Wishing I was closer to thee
Yet I'm so far from me
I can no longer even see the seashore
I just feel like a whore
I've prostituted fame and fortune and sold a dream that people could chase
To make another dollar to buy another drink- just call it the rat race

Why am I so empty? Aren't these things enough?

Am I no longer the guy who is tough, who is rough, who doesn't care, who is not fair?

Why am I no longer content? Why do I feel this void? It's like nothing on this earth can satisfy, not even the toys,

The toys of this world

Or looks of this girl

I'm confused?

I thought having all this would keep me amused?

Why is my soul longing for more than I have? Did I not attain more in my life than most would ever grab?

Help me, someone! Help me please! I'm losing myself! I'm losing this battle, I'm down on my knees!

Then it happened...

Someone so sweet pointed me to you! It was as if all the things I had could burn away, and I'd still be full!

What is this feeling? This feeling of peace and this state of rest

I can feel my heart beating out of my chest

It's not from being anxious and not from being depressed

Oh, it's because I am a son

Who no longer has to run

Because who the Son sets free is free indeed

Even if my mind can't catch up to the ways of thee

You saved me, but why?

I have lived more of my life living a lie

Telling people, I am happy when I really was not

Drinking away my problems, forget me not

You saw all that did, and you still chose me?

What did I do? To deserve a savior like you?

Nothing? I did nothing? How can that be?

Son, didn't I tell you that nothing can separate you from me.

Is that true? Do you really love that recklessly?

Son, can't you see? Reckless is My middle name

I am the God of order, yet I will not abstain
From reaching into hell to pull you out
I died on that cross, I won the bout
I rose from that grave, and it made them brave
To sacrifice my life to give you yours
Don't waste it, my son, I've called you for more
Don't be confused I'm talking to you
You that are holding this book
You that are wondering too
Is this God doing this for me?
I'm just reading some words, how can this be?
This can be because He is great
You didn't just get this book by some random fate
God is your Father and Jesus is King
Consider this book your wedding ring
He is ready to have you all to Him
Come to Him, now throw away your sins
They weren't yours before, so give them away
He is the God of closeness He doesn't lead you astray
He no longer wants you to be confused, you've been made a rarity
His ways are the opposite of confusion because all He wants is to give you... clarity
Be Free...

Read the Introduction...
-Derek

1

How It All Began

At the end of 2018, I was making my way out of a dark tunnel. Looking back now, this tunnel clearly had a light at the end, but I couldn't have said that during the time I was going through it. Time and yielding often position us to have the best reflection on the circumstances we go through. Let's get into the juice, shall we?

Time and yielding often position us to have the best reflection on the circumstances we go through.

Now you might be wondering who I am. Let me introduce myself.

My name is Derek Daniel Diaz. It's not a bad name, I think. *Thank you, Mom and Dad.* I was born on December 8th, 1989, at 3:10 in the morning, at St. Luke's Hospital in Manhattan, New York. I take real pride in saying that information to the detail. Do not ask me why. My family was living in New Jersey. By random chance, my mom went into labor in New York, so I got the title, *New Yorker—yeah baby!*

My childhood was like most others that grew up in the same area. I have many embarrassing photos with the most ghetto Big Bird and Cookie Monster costumes at my first birthday party. I have old photos to remind myself of my life while living in New York and Puerto Rico for vacation. Memories with those that have passed on are pretty much what's left of my family.

I have pictures of myself in second grade where I could have easily played a part in a *Harry Potter* film with how thick my glasses were. I was a cute kid.

For the rest of my childhood, I lived in Jersey City, New Jersey playing sports and getting into fights while hanging out at the mall, like your typical rough city kid.

My story doesn't have the common Christian climactic scenes of a hard life turning over completely to God. There is a glimmer of that sort of seasoned life—like my favorite *Sazón* Latino seasoning, before knowing Jesus. Trust me, there will be a time for those stories.

While I did have a crazy encounter, the heart of my story is centered around years after I decided to follow Jesus. That is why I believe this story is unique. We don't often hear of the biggest and most troubling time coming after an encounter with the Lord. After all, don't troubling times usually happen when you are completely exposed to the enemy from every direction, and you finally turn to God as a last resort? Ironically, whether it be during conversion (turning to God) or sanctification (growing in the faith), the end-result remains the same—getting to see God.

I'll be skipping over 24 years of my life for a very obvious reason that this is a book, not a novel. I hope to get straight to the point (for all the millennials) and begin from the night I got "saved."

* * *

It was Christmas Eve, 2013. I was living in Florida with my girlfriend at that time. I did *not* know the Lord and His ways, so this was very common to do for me. We had already been living together for about a year and a half, and I had a sudden unction to go to church. I mean, it was Christmas, and I was raised Catholic, so if there were ever a time to go to church, it would have been during Jesus' birthday (not validating its December 25th). Funny enough, I had a wild aunt who constantly invited me to go to church with her. Let's take a second to thank all the family that kept inviting us to church. *Praise you, Lord.*

It's only fitting that I describe her as wild because she was the only female security guard in a huge staff of men at a local megachurch. Wild, right?

She invited me that Christmas eve and I felt the nudge to go. The only problem was that my girlfriend didn't want to attend church. We had made plans to visit friends for a party, and she stuck to her plans. I recall as we both sat in our cars in the parking lot of our apartment complex looking into each other's eyes, time slowed down and I could tell something was going to change that night.

When I arrived at church, it was packed full of people. My aunt working security that night didn't spare any of her official titles and had me sit in the front row. *Like, really!* In a 2000-seat church, I repeat, I was dead center, front row. I couldn't remember most of that service, but at some point in the sermon, I dropped down to my knees weeping uncontrollably. I was weeping so much that my little cousin wasn't sure if I was mentally safe. Looking back now, it's a memory I can laugh about. My aunt, being amazing as she is, simply let me be.

At the end of the preaching, the pastor made an altar call for salvation, and that night, I accepted Jesus into my life. Right after the service, they were baptizing members in their courtyards. It only felt right to take the next step. So, I also baptized that night.

I feel that this book might be in the hands of someone who may not know Jesus and the Christian narrative, so I want to take some time to explain.

Allow me to preface the story of Jesus first with the truth about the Christian faith. Having faith to believe that Jesus is the Son of God does not require you to come to Jesus prepared to serve Him, unlike other religions. Working for Jesus does not prove your worthiness to be called a son or daughter. Jesus made you worthy the moment He chose to give His life on the cross, in exchange for yours. Even with a paragraph of information about the Christian faith, I ask that you allow one word to seep into your heart and soothe areas about what you believe God to be like, how you believe God operates, and why you don't believe God exists. And that word is **grace.**

Grace is the unmerited favor of God on humanity. It's simple really—His death opened the door for grace to flow into your heart to fill you with divine understanding and love. The love of Jesus is so set apart from other religions because of His invitation for you to believe that you are already with Him because of His work, and not yours. It is the only religion that screams faith over works, not works over faith. Just believe.

Grace is the unmerited favor of God on humanity.

Jesus didn't die for servants, He died for brothers and sisters. He made you worthy with His life, not the other way around. As you read these next few pages of the story of Jesus, I urge you not to get lost in your mind about what you already know, what you already think, and how you already feel. Allow the door of grace to swing wide open and see yourself walking through it. Experience His story with the understanding that all He went through was for you—yes, for you to experience freedom, joy, and peace. You are indeed good enough to be a part of His family.

Here are two realities that must burn inside of you. First, God is already pleased with who you are because He created you, so you do not need to try and "change." Second, just because you have not lived a life solely purposed to fulfill the will of God doesn't mean that God doesn't love you or still you call you son/daughter.

These two realities of Jesus bring us as humans to a place seeking answers to ideas that have been installed in our heads like hard drives. We have been taught that we have an unattainable God who judges people from heaven, looks at us through a microscope, and simply deems us not worthy. We assume heaven is empty, and hell is full because we can't measure up. The last part of that sentence might be true, but not because God is sending people to hell. He is only just honoring their choice.

He made you worthy with His life, not the other way around.

Jesus (Yeshua) was a man born for one purpose, you. The Bible says in Proverbs 8 that before the earth was made, Jesus was the sole delight of the Father, but when God created man, Jesus fell madly in love with man, and His sole desire was to be joined with us here on earth. For thousands of years, God entrusted the earth to us, man, but because of man's original sin, we slipped further and further away from the loving relationship God desired to have with us. God exercised every possible way to correct the problem. He promised people blessings and nations as long as they stayed in a relationship with Him, but man couldn't keep up his end of the deal. Specifically, God promised to dwell among us through a series of sacrifices as a way to enter into His presence. Over time, it was realized that the sacrifices of bull and sheep that men offered to God didn't change the condition of their hearts. Hence God became silent until the purposed time to do the one thing that could show the world and its human inhabitants that He meant His words saying, "nothing shall separate you from Me."

Born directly from God through Mary, Jesus came into this world to be Emmanuel (God With Us). Jesus' purpose was to live until the appointed time to reveal to His children (Israel) that He had come to redeem them from their ways and invite them into a loving relationship that He always desired for man to have. It wouldn't be done by power and strength, but by weakness and death.

Jesus' public ministry began when he was 30, where He taught in Jewish synagogues, walked among His people, healed the sick, cleansed people lost from the ways of the world, and showed people of like faith the true power that lay in a relationship with God. The Bible accounts that we were the joy set before Him when He died on the cross (Hebrews 12:2). The verse begins to unlock a passion you can see in no other religion. Jesus delighted in you, coming to earth to be with you, knowing you were the joy set before Him, which gave Him the strength to endure the cross, with the reality that even with that display of love, you still have a choice to not choose Him or love Him back.

Prior to Him getting to the cross, He was accused of blaspheming God, meaning people stuck to what they read in the Scriptures, but they couldn't interpret what Jesus was saying about God. Therefore, He must have been mocking or disrespecting God because He spoke contrary to what they knew. Jesus was never apart from God the Father, so He spoke about Him with a love and passion others didn't comprehend.

Additionally, He was falsely charged for crimes He didn't commit. Instead of fighting to be proven innocent, He left the decision to be crucified up to the people He created at the beginning of time. Jesus in the Gospel of John is referred to as the Word of God made flesh, we can flip all the way back to Genesis 1 to see how the very breath of God is what filled Adam's lungs as he was the first man to walk the earth. After standing in silence before Pontius Pilate and the Israelites showing enough evidence of who He truly was, men decided to hang Him on a cross. The very people He came to set free from their ways put Him on the cross to be slain. This was part of the Master plan.

The Bible states that had the rulers of this present world order had known what would come after Jesus' death, they wouldn't have prompted man to kill Him (1 Cor 2:8). Jesus was betrayed, gossiped about, falsely accused, denied innocence, and killed for crimes He didn't commit. Consider His death and resurrection the final seal of approval.

For thousands of years, the Jewish nation once a year on the "Day of Atonement" would sacrifice a lamb on behalf of the people's sin, done by the village's high priest to grant forgiveness for all the sin committed that year. Jesus was God's answer to the ritual sacrifice to allow one last sacrifice to be made on behalf of all of humanity. Jesus was the perfect lamb, the unblemished, perfect sacrifice worthy to atone all men present and future to redeem humanity back into His relationship with God. The Bible says God poured out all His wrath on Jesus so that you and I can experience the grace of our loving Father.

When we chose Jesus, we choose life; we choose love and we are chosen to remain in His family forever. Jesus took all our sin, disease, curses, mental illness, shame, and judgment of the sins we committed and nailed all that nasty junk there with Him on the cross. This not only implies how much we were worth to Him, but it negates the often-made assumption that God doesn't understand us.

The Bible goes on to say that He understands humanity, for as a Man He was tempted in every way just as we are, and conquered sin (Hebrews 4:15). Not just on the cross but in His actual life. As I mentioned earlier about the high priest offering sacrifice on behalf of the people, another part of his role was to hear out the sins of the people on a daily basis, so that when he went before the Lord, he knew how to pray for his people. Similarly, Jesus is making prayers for you before the Father as your personal High Priest (Romans 8:34).

As He promised to His disciples while He was alive, on the third day, He rose from the grave of His death, and our God - the resurrected Jesus, promised all those who believe in Him and submit to the ways of the Kingdom of God would indeed have the same life He had and even a better one. His life, traded for mine and yours. God chose you from the moment you took a breath to be included in His story, regardless of where you are right now.

The Gospels in the New Testament display in detail the death and resurrection of Jesus. The act of water baptism is the very gesture Jesus displayed on the cross. When we submerge ourselves into the water, we tell the world publicly that the old man/woman is no longer alive and that person has died with Christ (Romans 6). When we come out of the water, we join in His resurrection with new life and the Spirit that God promised us.

The Holy Spirit within us is perfect because He is the Spirit of God, but we still have to renew our minds, will, and emotions daily (our soul) by reading and meditating on the Bible as the Psalmist says in chapter 77 of the Psalms. This daily process is called sanctification—the walking out of our faith. We may believe, but any relationship not invested into can become dull and dry. It is the same with our relationship with God. God's goal is to commune with you as a friend to a friend. He listens to your voice better than no other and will always speak to us with compassion, even in correction. The more you read the Word of God, the more you will know who you really are (made in the image of God), and in return, you give Him more space to dwell inside of you.

The Apostle Paul puts it this way in Romans 8:1, *"there is therefore now no condemnation to those who are in Christ Jesus, who do not walk according to the flesh, but according to the Spirit."* So, I speak to you to believe in these words. If it is evidence for validity, Jesus has it; if it's an encounter that is tangible, Jesus has it; if it's a requirement of knowing, without a doubt, you are forgiven, loved, and pleasing to the Creator of the universe, Jesus has it. I will go on to add in full faith that no other way will satisfy your spirit and soul. No other religion offers answers to all of life's questions. Jesus is the way, the truth, and the life, and I say confidently that no man may come to the Father unless through Him (Jesus).

After reading this book, if you have decided to follow Jesus, or you have been walking with Him, but you have never joined Him in total obedience and surrender, don't wait. The freedom He exchanges is like no other. Don't wait for the church Sunday when they baptize or the right tide in the ocean; it can be done anywhere and with anyone doing the initiation (See Acts 8:26-40). He loves you! He loves you! He loves you! I can't even begin to explain the love He has for you.

In Song of Songs 4:9, He professes that *"you reach into my heart.*

With one flash of your eyes, I am undone by your love, my beloved, my equal, my bride. You leave me breathless." This is just a glimpse of his adoration toward you. The Word of God is filled with love notes from God, wanting not just your surrender, but to fill your heart with real tangible love.

He is the best friend you always wanted, the perfect soulmate you long for. He satisfies all things and brings all things unto Him. I pray that you join Him now while you still have the will to choose Him. One day the decision might be already made up for you. I leave this excerpt with something I have marked my life with; "Jesus lived the life I could not live and died the death I should have died, so if He died for me, I'll live for Him."

Shortly after my water baptism, I returned home feeling like a new man with a new purpose and a new destiny. What were my thoughts—to be a better man and boyfriend to my lady. What were His plans? To get me out of that relationship as quickly as He could.

Being naïve, I spent the following seven months doing everything I could to make it work. We tried celibacy, attending services together, and Bible studies. I found myself trying to modify my behaviors instead of allowing God to renew the man on the inside and thinking if I changed this and that I will be considered better, which was not the case. All Jesus wanted was a surrendered heart. So, within a matter of days, after our 2nd anniversary, I found myself alone and heartbroken in a big apartment, wondering how I got there and realizing there was no turning back.

This is the part of my life where I can say I had the first actual encounter with the Lord, but I didn't know that the encounter was even Jesus or that it meant to seek more of Him.

From a very early age, I had a really bad addiction to pornography. Some sexual abuse and access to the internet can jack up a kid's life. Well, there I was, all alone in my apartment, and the fear of loneliness crept in, and I went to do what I knew best. As I was about to turn to another webpage, a bright white light took over my entire computer screen and lit my living room up completely. And as if I was in a trance, my fingers led me to YouTube. I created a channel that night and found my Bible, which I add I had never read. I opened it to Proverbs. I hit the record button, read Proverbs 1, and taught it to the screen as if I was some grand scholar. It wasn't that great. That video is still public today.

From the very night that she left home, I developed a hunger and pursuit to make videos for the Lord. Taking everyday topics, things I read in the Bible, and blending them, making videos for people to hear, was all I felt led to do. I put my head down and started serving the Lord. Life was good. That time of my life was in July 2014.

Somewhere during my time at church, I was told that dating around wasn't the best thing to do. Simple and practical advice that a man like me did need to hear around that time. So, I took the advice they lent out. *"Date the girl you see; marry the girl you date."* This is the advice I will not give you today, but I am only replaying this for context purposes. The advice I would give you today, which is quoted from a very good friend of mine, is simple: *"I'd rather wait than date."*

I'd rather wait than date.

While I don't believe that the previous statement was the actual heart of the church, I have come to realize that in a lot of instances, even with the right heart and intentions, if I don't have a solid foundation with God and His truth, my view of life choices will always be skewed and led from people's perspectives and not God's. Churchgoers are not hypocrites; they are mostly honest God-seeking people that often don't have a true revelation of how God sees things in this world. I add this because somehow we (the world) made Christians out to be perfect, and when they act up, we cast the blame on God asking how can He be real if Christians messed up again? There is no reason to blame the church and anyone in particular for the advice, however, that statement got to me and changed my perspective on dating.

In September 2014, I noticed a girl in the church working on videos, similar to what I was doing. She was making videos, providing daily motivation, and putting them on social media. This was a very similar approach I was taking. So, taking some friends' advice, I decided to pursue a friendship, which led to dating.

From the outside looking in, she had what I would say, the life I always wanted. She had a corner house with a mom and dad, a close brother, and she grew up with loving and caring supervision that had Godly influence. It's beautiful to see the influence Christian parents have on Christian children. To be completely honest, I came from brokenness. It sounds cruel to say this because when my parents read this, they'll think otherwise since they believe they gave me a great life. I know they did the best they could, and I can't deny it. Looking back, there were areas I couldn't be helped any more than I was at the time. It was simply due to a lack of familiarity with the Christian upbringing on their part and rebellion on my part. The Christian transformation is from the inside out, not outside in; that's the soul part I mentioned above. Even if my circumstances had been different or even the best in the world's eyes, my heart still would not have been any better.

At nine years old, my parents separated. My mom and I moved into a tiny two-bedroom apartment, which would be considered section 8 housing, and our rooms were separated with a plastic curtain. I lived there for the rest of my teenage life. I took that living situation and made myself a victim. There was no hope for a better life in my eyes or even a foundation of God, so why wouldn't I blame and shame everything on my parents for the condition we found ourselves in. I was raised with great parents, yet each of them didn't really use Christian principles to raise me. They raised me how they both saw fit, and anyone else who watched me also had an influence on my life because I didn't know any better. So rather than rooting myself in one truth with my eyes fixed on one hope. I wandered around like a person being tossed in the waves most of my young life taking any advice from people I believed had their best interest in me. I tell you this part of my story because you must understand how roots develop. They start in the soil long before any signs of growth appear. Both the good and the bad roots. The way I saw life at 9-years-old directly impacted the very situation I found myself in at

29-years-old. Twenty years later with a ton of life experience and chaos, I still couldn't find a place to be grounded.

Okay, back to the woman I was dating. I was looking forward to what she had to offer my life outside of herself; in other words, her good family, the hope for connection to something bigger. What a skewed way to start a relationship, right? Our relationship was somewhat pushed toward the limelight and rushed. This is something we both can agree on now if asked. Our own individual lives and volunteering together in the church put us in front of many people very fast, and normalcy left as quickly as "fame" crept in. After ten months of dating, we got engaged, and ten months later, we got married. Every step of the way was a battle, and we both failed to see certain red flags that should have told us to wait.

I believe that love is a choice, to first get into a relationship, and a continual choice to make daily. Love is not fully roses and blossoms; there also thorns that couples will face together. When two people become one, the beauty of facing the trials together is that they both understand they can do it together, not separately. In reality, it is the thorns that make love real. Marriage is 100% each individual giving all of themselves away and never expecting anything in return. Why? Because you have found yourself so deeply moved by this person that nothing they do would cause you to consider another option. It sounds a lot like Jesus' love for us.

> **Marriage is 100% each individual giving all of themselves away and never expecting anything in return.**

A loving couple that has lasted fifty beautiful years together doesn't last that long by avoiding trials and relying solely on what the world calls happiness. Love is showing up day in and day out and making it through the very reasons you said I do in the first place.

Weddings come with a warning to the bride and groom. We just don't see it. We, as officiants, ask them both, do you take this man/woman to be your... why? Because we are praying they both see that your I do is covering a multitude of circumstances and a wide array of situations that can turn that whole I didn't sign up for this mentality on really fast. We must believe that if God has given us this person, we choose to die to even our happiness in the belief that God will be glorified in it.

You might be thinking, *Derek, why get married if I'm not even happy?* I'm not saying you won't be happy. I'm saying your decision to be married is not rooted in how the person makes you feel, but rather the ability God has given this person to bring out the best version of you for the world to see. This is what differentiates the people who marry that have already cultivated a close relationship with God as a single person and would rather see Him glorified through their life rather than someone who constantly is looking to please themselves with someone else and then depend on that person to bring them all the satisfaction, joy and happiness that unfortunately can't be attained by one person outside of God himself.

> *I'm saying your decision to be married is not rooted in how the person makes you feel, but rather the ability God has given this person to bring out the best version of you for the world to see.*

Another important factor that did get us to the altar sooner was that her dad's recovery after suffering from Sickle Cell Anemia. We feared his symptoms wouldn't have allowed him to walk her down the aisle, let alone be there. He was a walking miracle, though. Doctors gave him only years to live, but he surpassed all odds and lived well beyond the doctors' expectations. I don't want to paint him as a crutch to getting to the altar, but we both wanted him to see and enjoy a joyous moment.

In August 2016, we got married and moved into our first apartment, hoping that we did enough premarital counseling and marriage retreat seminars to get through what everyone said would be the tough first year. Little did we know everything we read and everything we attended didn't prepare us for what was coming our way.

2

A Dream Come True

The church I was saved in and met my wife was considered a super evangelical church. The kind of church people would call "seeker" friendly. The term seeker means someone who doesn't know Jesus but might be interested to know. We created enough sparkle to attract people into the building, sometimes to the point they don't realize it's a church. The goal was to make the church an attraction, and Jesus was the superstar.

The church was big in promoting how Jesus can bring you a better life. Now, I am not discounting that method nor that truth, but do you remember when I shared about my baptism? The act of submerging myself meant I felt a holy conviction (utterly convinced) to live a life submitted to the Lordship of Jesus. In other words, I believed that Jesus' ways of living were not only the right way but also beneficial for my life and the life of others prior to going into the water.

To be honest, I didn't feel the call to submit fully to Christ that Christmas night. I'm sure some people can walk through Christianity without the weight of the cross and try to change their behavior as best as they know, but often when a demonic strategy comes to knock you off your balance and gets to your doorstep because of a behavior change and not a life surrendered, it makes you feel as if all of your work was for nothing. And we as humans try to fix problems that were meant for Jesus to handle (Matthew 11:28-29). This, in turn, is why I had such a hard time during the moments that will shortly follow these chapters.

There is a common saying around the Christian community which is that *"the Lord is interested in heart transformation, not behavior modification."* If I would have truly meditated on that phrase, I could have avoided a lot of trials throughout my marriage. This leads me to our first couple of months of marriage.

About 2 months after the honeymoon, we started to get on track with paying down debt, work-life, and balancing the newlywed life. I put on the honeymoon weight and gained 15 lbs. *Thank you, Royal Caribbean.* I needed to get myself in better shape, and in November decided to join some friends playing basketball, looking to both make it a sport I enjoy playing, but also an intentional workout routine for me.

On the first night going to play after about the 2nd game, I went down hard, twisting my left ankle. Thankfully, the park shut down as I was about to try and muster through it. The pain was far more excruciating than normal so the drive home was extremely painful. I drove a stick shift car so, pressing down the clutch pedal to shift gears made it all worse.

When I got home, I needed the TLC any hubby would want, and we assumed it would get better over time. Thankfully, Thanksgiving was right around the corner, so I would have time off to rest up. When my foot swelled up to the size of a pool ball after about a week of being off of it, we knew it was time to go visit an orthopedic surgeon. After the MRI, it was confirmed I had actually torn my Achilles tendon, and it was a full tear.

Shortly after that, the surgeon I chose ran through the scenarios of what the next 6 to 9 months of our lives would look like. I had two options, to either get surgery or lock myself in a permanent cast to heal the tendon naturally. He gave us a week to decide and a follow-up MRI.

One day that week while watching YouTube videos with a friend, we stumbled across a white preacher with dreads praying for people in the streets and God healing them. We had no idea who this man was, but we were both hooked. We continued to watch sermons and then more testimonials of his ministry. After our wives got home that night, we felt impressed to put to practice our new-found faith. We saw instant healing in his wife right after we prayed. My friend and our wives prayed over my ankle in faith, and when we went back to the surgeon to do the follow-up MRI, the tendon was fully put back together. It was like a lightbulb went off in my mind and I wondered why no one had ever told me before that God heals our physical bodies too.

The doctor was astonished by the news he saw from the report and told me the only thing left for me to do was wear a temporary boot for about 3 to 6 months to make sure the tendon healed properly.

I am telling you this short story because, in the midst of something really eye-opening and amazing done by the Lord, there was a big turning point in my marriage that happened right around the same time.

We wound up prolonging writing out and sending our thank you cards from the wedding because of all we had been doing once we got married and the injury. Trying to fill these cards out with a laid-up foot didn't make matters better for me. That time in our lives put a lot of stress on the marriage and while I started to listen to sermons and get a perspective that pointed to spiritual attacks on our marriage, my partner did not see it that way. She saw all the natural issues going on and it made our arguments really difficult to ever get over.

Shortly after that time, by the turn of the new year of 2017, we already started having the D-conversation a.k.a *divorce*. This is the first part about transparency I want to address with you all. My marriage was in no way over by 2017, but we needed help. Rather than looking to each other and the pastor that offered us to go and plant the church with him, we should have worked on our marriage first. We took the call to go because we both felt it was a great opportunity to grow in our own callings. *This part will matter later. You might feel I just dropped you off a cliff because I didn't even explain the D-conversation, but don't worry. You'll get enough to paint the picture without it.*

Getting to the beginning of the new year took a lot of strength because we already couldn't see how to mend arguments and get past differences. And putting the obstacles of church planting on top of it made that time even more difficult. I don't mean that the specific experience of this church plant was extra difficult; it's the process of planting in general. If anyone has ever planted a garden you can easily understand this point. You must first dig that hole. The first area that can get difficult is not having the right tool.

Now you might say, *Derek who doesn't own a shovel,* and to my response, I'd say *you'd be surprised.* Using the wrong tool can even make the digging to plant the seed strenuous. After laying the seed in the ground you may feel that the hard work is over but it literally only just begun. Now comes the daily routine of watering and waiting.

Watering the ground when nothing comes forth can tire you out emotionally. *I'll stop here, so I don't go off on a whole sermon, but I wanted to give you context to what my wife and I decided to step into despite knowing we had issues we needed to rectify internally in our marriage.*

Although America is the land of opportunity, the pursuit for more becomes vain if we do not change our ways. We learn to put on a face when we are seeking a better job, even if we are lazy, unengaged, and bad employees. We take on new opportunities with no means of managing the new responsibilities, leaving us in a vicious cycle of helpless vanity. Until we can allow God to work out things within us we will continue to drift and never truly grow.

> **Until we can allow God to work out things within us, we will continue to drift and never truly grow.**

Ministry, YouTube, traveling, and gifts (material items) distracted us both, enough to a place of tolerance without having to actually face some really deep-rooted issues we needed to talk about. The funny thing about the enemy is that he is at the root of the problems in marriages, and he is also at the root of distracting couples from facing them.

We knew that we each had deep problems we needed to face individually, but we didn't want to address them. Even worse, we didn't know how to. We kept layering on masks of happiness that slowly got pulled back every time a trial came our way. Because we found a "new thing" to keep us happy whether, in the form of a toy (gadget), or a destination, we put the smile back on over and over. I will say the biblical foundation to a healthy marriage starts with the husband, and I did not possess what it took to maintain that responsibility.

The funny thing about the enemy is that he is the root of the problems in marriage; and he is also the root of the distractions of facing them.

Chapter 5 of Paul's letter to Ephesus speaks to how husbands must love their wives as Christ loved the church—sacrificing Himself for His Bride. Though He CAN and WILL lead her, he wanted to show her that even His life was worth giving up for her. The husband also must stay in a relationship with the Father because it is on the Father to provide direction for the marriage on the paths to which He knows best will Glorify Him. Paul uses phrases such as showering your wife with the Word of God, which metaphorically means the cleansing of her soul with the Word of the Lord (The Bible). Words to the scripture I knew but still lived with a "me" mentality. If she wasn't making me happy, why should I bother? I thought my marriage was to make me happier, and if it wasn't, I was not too concerned with fixing it. These were the thoughts that rummaged around my brain constantly, which caused a huge wall to come up anytime God wanted to start healing our marriage.

The fact about a godly marriage is simple, you aren't in it for yourself. The blessing of a godly marriage is that two individuals will selflessly give away all they are to their spouse because serving to them was always better than receiving. They both know they are filled with the love of Jesus and so that they both do not expect the other to fill a void because Jesus already did it. I am not saying at all that Godly marriages don't fight, bicker, and get into dark times, what I am trying to conclude is that in the realm of marriage, even when those times come, they both can run to the father on their own, take their offenses to Him, and He can mend wounds, so they can return to each other in love. Paul talks often about living righteously and I thought that to be again something that regarded the way I behaved rather than seeing my life and hers as God sees it. Filled with compassion and love, considering her over myself, choosing to always be humble. Certain responsibilities are given to the man of the house who listens to the head of the house - Jesus.

I did not have the full understanding of that responsibility, and honestly, I didn't want to do it. When I was doing it I was definitely not doing it to please the Lord and His desire for marriage. I did it for selfish reasons to get my way. I still felt like I deserved to be happy first; then to serve her. The problem is that when two individuals both feel like they deserve something that they believe can only come from the other, they're both left never getting it. Setting expectations in marriage is dangerous when we don't become fully satisfied with Jesus. Depending on our upbringing and reaction to the world, being let down can cause a lot of damage and hurt. My natural reaction would be to shut down and isolate (pretty hard to do in marriage I might add), in the worst of conditions I would seek emotional support from friends, rather than my wife. You can see how on my side alone the tendencies I had could cause a lot of hurt and pain in the marriage, so imagine also adding her ways of how she reacted to pain and stress, they were both recipes for disaster. We did not understand about receiving full satisfaction from a relationship with the Father, so we left all the responsibility to each other, never realizing it was never our role to fulfill.

In September 2017, the church was finally launching. It was a proud moment for us and the group of people that pulled together to make this church plant happen were finally about to see the fruit of all of the hard work of focusing on and engaging in the city we knew little about. For my marriage, it was quite the opposite. We both knew the cost but failed to fully understand the weight that was going to be placed on our relationship, and it sent us in a whirlwind for the first couple of months of the church plant.

The launch meant long weekends for us, driving an hour to church and back, which was over 50 miles away. We were also a set-up and tear-down church; which meant that the facility we rented had to be set up to look like the church before people arrived and placed back to its original condition after we finished. A typical weekend for us consisted of arriving on Saturday nights and working for two to three hours to set up the church, then showing up again at 8:00 AM on Sunday, and not leaving until 2:00 PM.

By December 2017, the effects of the church were wearing us down. Not to mention in my personal life, I walked through a big issue in my job that resulted in me leaving the job for the remaining three months of 2017. To say that pressure was on us is an understatement. The fighting and ineffectiveness of our communication were both at an all-time high. We were super connected to the church, but somehow still struggled to maintain a healthy relationship with each other, while serving the body. We sought the advice of many people—those that walked in our shoes before us, and those walking in it with us. It didn't seem like anything was assisting the issue. It wasn't the effectiveness of their advice it was actually the posture of my heart (so that I don't speak for her) I did not want to commit to change. I would start a trend of getting better but then immediately go right back when an offense built up.

One of the problems in our relationship was I always wanted to be right. I consistently saw the right and wrong in various situations and pointed fingers to cast blame, so she could feel "less of a Christian." I wanted to shine independently, rather than build her up to shine with me. As a union, we were helpless, but alone, I was killing it, or so I thought.

I regularly felt in competition with her even though I never voiced it. I wanted favor in the sight of the Lord and was willing to hurt the one closest to me to feel as if I deserved it.

The Bible teaches us that the Lord is a respecter of no person, (Romans 2:11) which in lay terms means He doesn't favor one over the other because of our works. In the context of a relationship with God and/or marriage, we are all His children. He gives us His all-encompassing love that is never-ending and full at all times. His love is equally measured to every individual, and is given away to where we couldn't look to the left or to the right and say, *"I have more than you."* I had an orphan mindset (looking at life from a place of lack), so even the smallest signs of favor she received from the Lord manipulated my view of her and of the Lord. I can trace back to the biggest blow was knowing she was given an official title at the church while I was still just considered a volunteer. How petty I was. It's a deafening issue that needs to be addressed because the enemy is always taking even the good things of the Lord and tainting them to get his way. We must view the Father correctly because if not, we will view the gifts He gives to His children selfishly and miss out on the true blessing He has for us.

We must view the Father correctly, because if not, we will view the gifts He gives to His children selfishly and miss out on the true blessing He has for us.

I obviously can't address the whole issue here in this book but to add to this based on my marriage I can give you this context. God is interested in you being whole. The Bible says in Romans 8:22 that the earth is groaning for sons & daughters, i.e. men and women who know exactly who they are and more importantly know who's they are. It creates confidence that nothing nor no one can replace where God is. The world has us convinced that our mate will complete us which is not the case. God's desire is to see His children come to a place of knowing fully that He satisfies all of our desires and needs because He can and will if we allow Him to. Wholeness is the definition of Holiness in a nutshell. We are called to be Holy but how can we if we depend on things from people or material here on earth. Only God can truly fulfill that void in us at all times and in all circumstances. What I'm trying to get at is wait… wait upon Him to bring to you what you need in life not what you want. He can bring you to a place of not wavering to the left or to the right when a guy or girl walks into your life, or a job opportunity arises that might be good. You can be rooted in Him to a place where no matter what comes, you know it will not add to anything you already have with Him. Instead, you will either see it as an opportunity to grow you closer to God or to distract you from His purpose over your life.

One of the big differences I saw earlier on was that my relationship with my wife was built upon chemistry and not compatibility. Chemistry is the glue that starts the building process of relationships. Compatibility is the silent pure love that has rooted in each individual that doesn't require affection or adoration to be confirmed by someone else. We both had strong chemistry because of what we both desired, but any time an opportunity arose to present how compatible we were with each other, it fell grossly short of what we saw in other godly marriages.

While we were still engaged, we attended a marriage conference and one part of the retreat was building a mission statement to which we couldn't agree on one. Funny enough, when that same couple hosted another conference a year later into our marriage, the same question arose, and we couldn't bring ourselves to agree on a mission statement again for our marriage.

Now you might say Derek, *it's not that big of a deal*, but as believers, it really should be. We, as Christians, do not marry simply to become happy. That is a backward way of getting into a union. Marriage is one of the key ways we get to glorify God through our lives. Through something greater than our happiness is our service unto the Lord as a union that ultimately gives Him delight and joy.

I want to remind you that God's first desire is to see you as a son or daughter who is fully content in who He is. Rather than focusing your attention on fixing your marriage, first, bring yourself to the Lord. The more you work with Him through lies that have been spoken over you, you will begin to see a change in your relationships because you took the attention off others and focused on growing yourself.

I say this not to discourage where you are spiritually or emotionally but to simply remind you that Jesus gave his life so I can find full satisfaction in Him. I didn't give my life to Him, so I can get anything more than he already gave. Likewise, in marriage we commit our wholeness individually to a greater cause which is to let the world in on a secret about God (Jesus) He loves; love, because He is LOVE. He delights in our union being whole because it fulfills a purpose in the kingdom to represent what His union is like to us. His union is never-ending, unconditional, always serving, always loving, and most importantly willing to suffer. We have not been taught some of those principles until we ask them to be recited at the altar on our wedding day. It's scary, but it's true.

He gave His life, so I CAN give mine, I didn't give my life to Him, so I can get anything more than He already gave.

If you are a believer reading this, I want to encourage you to take all the verses you've already laid out for your wedding day and practice them now. Practice them with yourself and God. Practice them with your friends and family. What would it look like for you to represent love now in your singleness before you get to the altar to not allow the euphoria of the day mistake the true sacrifice marriage is called to be?

Don't take this chapter and think, *oh there's literally no fun in Christian marriages.* That's not true. In fact, the fun and joy in the marriage are the complete pieces of the union. Having a God-centered marriage with a mission to serve and glorify God together while building a beautiful life, full of memories and fun are all the contributing factors that make the essence of what kingdom marriages should encompass.

So, I urge you to throw out any lies that are trying to convince you that you know why Christian marriages don't last. The first lie is that a marriage centered around God is not a healthy one. And the second, having a marriage focused on building God's Kingdom doesn't mean you miss out on life. Wanting someone else to make you happy is unreliable, but finding happiness in each other, now that's something we can hold on to for life.

3

Thought the Grass Would Be Greener

There is not a storm you walk into that the Lord is not prepared to walk through with you. God's deliverance system is to walk you through things; not get you out of them, according to Psalm 23. David's song to the Lord was one that had unique confidence that even though he knew he was in the middle of an issue, he trusted that God was going to lead him through it. He knew that if he simply let God lead, his soul would find the rest he was looking for. In that rest, he would eventually find himself on the other side of all that trial and pain and be able to look back and say God brought him through it all. To say the least, I needed to know these things in my own heart.

> *There is not a storm you walk into that the Lord is not prepared to walk through with you. God's deliverance system is to walk you through things; not get you out of them.*

The start of 2018 was a good one. I had been asked by my lead pastor to kick off the new year, teaching the congregation, which meant I would finally be able to recite a sermon that didn't end in the ABCs of salvation. *For all those children's pastors out there—you know what I'm talking about.*

Stepping into a pastoral call was a dream for me. There was also an exciting buzz around the church because we were about to launch our young adult's ministry and have it swing into full effect in February.

As the young adult's ministry grew from its start in February, it catapulted the strength of the church in just a few months. We partnered with a local coffeehouse in the neighborhood mall and met there on Saturday nights to hold our services. Together with another young pastor, we co-led from March to June in that space. We saw an amazing wave of young people that met every Saturday night to grow deeper in the Word, then show up Sunday morning and not just attend service, but serve the body in many different ways.

Around March 2018, we took a step of faith and moved up north of the town we ministered in, leaving our family and all we knew. Now, when I say a step of faith, it really was a step of faith because we had no jobs. She was going to waitress at a new local restaurant near our new home. While we had no income, we were believing that God would provide for us financially.

It wasn't until June that I landed a bank job placing us at a financial advantage. Unfortunately, it was at the same time that our venue for our ministry at the coffee shop in the mall shut down. We needed to find a new location to meet.

God had blessed our marriage with a spacious townhome and with some convincing, I got the "Mrs." to agree to host the Bible study group in our home.

Growing up in a single mother home and an only child, much of my youth was spent in front of a computer screen or TV playing video games. Trying to cultivate fake friendships through chat rooms or fantasizing about what life should look like through movies and games was how I spent most of my young childhood. When I look back on that time in my life I realize that my identity was found in anything that called me accepted. Whether gangs, wrestling, movies, you name it, and I jumped on that train. I didn't know who I was and I wasn't about to miss out on the next best thing for that reason. The void in my heart would eventually bring strife to our marriage.

As we hosted the meetings in our home, we agreed to set in place some parameters such as a curfew for people to leave so my wife and I had our own individual time, but I selfishly pursued the acceptance from outside

25

friendships. Growing up, I was always left out and any friendships I had were more of a one on one friendship; so, when there were large gatherings – even with the family, I would never want to leave. I loved the chaos of a full home. It seemed like everything was smooth, but then the enemy crept in.

I became distracted in my marriage and used ministry and the new life with many great friends as a reason to stay distracted. Also, I was not used to being the center of authority and attention. My life consisted of playing team sports and always feeling like the guy that was good, but not the best. I may have dominated my sport at the time but I wasn't at all dominating life. I wasn't the person people wanted to hang with.

I was so far from understanding my own truth and identity that the way people reacted to me defined my mood and character. I now know this was far from Gospel-centered living. My need was and is still Jesus. My dependence is in Him alone. I am not in any requirement of people to validate me. This place of lack caused me to view the current situation I found myself in with a group of young people excited for God, excited for community, and excited for what I was saying. This excitement pulled me in a direction where I chased after them and not Him.

To make matters worse, my wife and I began working opposite schedules. When we finally did get time together, it was either serving the church or very late at night. We were no longer living together, but cohabitating.

The problem is not always the tension. It's when both parties know there is an overlying tension and they each choose to cope with it and live life around it. It's a sense of defeat and a lack of desire to change. It's telling God, *"this situation I'm in has no hope and I've given up even the willingness to fight to make it better."*

The problem is not always the tension. It's when both parties know there is an overlying tension and chooses to cope with it and live life around it.

In the effort to restore our marriage, we spent money on books, trips, marriage retreats, and even Christian counseling. *To be frank, it was not worth the money.*

As it says in Proverbs 11:14, *"Where there is no counsel, the people fall."* Good counsel is important. Any counsel that is not led by the Holy Spirit and the full truth of the Gospel can lead people astray.

We inevitably got to the place of being done with trying to help the cause of restoring our marriage; and we both faded away into doing life, alone yet together. From June to September, it was a haze of the same thing week in and week out. *Work, church, serve, movie, sleep, rinse and repeat.*

Shortly after the church celebrated its 1st-year anniversary, the young adult ministry invested in multiple copies of a specific book that impacted me personally., We even purchased a study guide and a DVD series diving deep into a study on the book. Every week, we opened our meeting with a song from Upperroom called *"Surrounded."* The words took us into a deeper understanding of God and our position in our lives that very few of us had ever received. From September to December, we saw a huge breakthrough in our young adult members. Real, honest conversations were happening and people were being set free from the pain they experienced from their own church upbringing.

During that time, my co-leader asked to take a 3-month sabbatical for healing purposes, meaning I had to take charge of leading the group. This pushed me and my wife further from each other as I gave more time to the ministry. I blame myself because I failed to even ask her if she wanted to be included in things that were going on with the study. *Remember my issue with wanting to shine.*

Deep within me, I carried deep envy of other relationships in ministry and their marriages. Exodus 20:17 says *"Thou shall not covet thy neighbor's wife,"* yet here I was watching other pastors preach and how their wives responded to their sermons, eager to write notes and remaining present and attentive.

I tried to manipulate that same feeling by hiding all I was learning in order to teach it publicly and hope she would one day admire me. I was secretly afraid that she would somehow reject me because she knew everything I knew—or even worse—knew more than I did.

I recall a night I was teaching at the home. I was in the middle of teaching and paused for almost 15 seconds and stared at my wife; because I knew she was on her phone scrolling through social media—completely checked out. In her mind, I was not fulfilling my end of the marriage covenant and not holding true to the duties laid out for husbands in the Bible so, I had no right to teach others how to live out the Gospel. I was being so hypocritical in my own walk, there was no reason I should have been teaching. There was much truth to that during that time and I take responsibility for how I was not the greatest husband.

She attempted to speak to me about these gaps. Knowing I was still trapped with the needing to be happy physiologically, I cut all her attempts short. Noticing that disconnect that night changed a lot in me. It stung deeply. While I had young men and women of God being impacted by the way the Lord was using me, the closest person to me was so uninterested in what I had to say that she tuned me out completely and the whole room knew it. If I wasn't aware my marriage was in turmoil before, I knew it then perfectly. She was checked out and it fueled more indifference with me. Honestly, I couldn't have lifted another finger to care. This was a deep-rooted issue that neither one of us wanted to address. I was so unmotivated to continue and she was simply frustrated because she was trying to show me that we needed change. I want to urge those reading who find themselves relating to this story now to pause.

The Apostle Paul writes in 1 Corinthians 13:4 and opens this wonderful text about love by saying first, love suffers long. Take a moment to just sit in that. We as a human race have emphasized what love ought to be like, and suffering is not one of them. We as believers know and understand that Jesus died on the cross and suffered because He loved us, but when did that type of love stop? This brings the question to mind, do you love Him or do you like what He did for you? It is now so evident in me that my view of love was so selfish I couldn't even grasp the reality of what it meant to be in love. Love is not the good times and the laughs only.

Love is when one spouse loses their job and the burden to carry the finances of the home falls on the other. Love is when one gets sick and hospitalized and the other is joined to them in the room for months until they're better.

Love is the trial and the hardship of the union while choosing and knowing that a brighter day is coming. Why? Because the first representative of love is that it suffers. I'm saying this because as a husband, I disconnected love with suffering and proved to myself that suffering meant there wasn't any love to have. I didn't want to move in the direction of healing because I believed it was ultimately broken and it was not beneficial for me. It's my generation's curse as a whole, rather than fix we throw away and buy new. A social and habitual pandemic of never fully believing in the beauty of choosing love over and over again. I am saying all this because it is who I was at the time and I urge you to not fall into that trap as I did.

Love is the trial and the hardship of the union while choosing and knowing that a brighter day is coming.

The enemy wants to make you believe you were right in your doubts, make you believe there's always better, and that life shouldn't look this way. Now, there are certain scenarios I am not addressing in this short book, but simple fights and arguments I am covering here. Ask God to speak to you about the areas of your life you still hold on to that you feel you need things to be done to your benefit and ask Him how to give that away to Him. When two people can spend their life believing that giving is better than receiving, it opens such beauty for the Lord to work miracles and wonders in each of the individual's hearts. Suffering and sacrifice are the fruit of a life surrendered to God and a marriage unto Him. Not because it is the only representation of a surrendered love. When the good times, the laughs, the joy, and the utter union you have shines alongside it, the world gets to see God in every form of your union. They won't believe the lie that Christians have this perfect marriage and that God is unattainable because their marriage or life doesn't look that way.

Suffering and sacrifice are the fruit of a life surrendered to God and a marriage unto Him.

So, please pause and reflect when you can. I made this book because I want people to focus on themselves wherever they are, and focus on their pursuit of God rather than run back to the very thing He picked them up from.

4

My Worst Fears Come True

I know it may sound harsh when I say I didn't care that my marriage was in turmoil, but it was my honest truth. I won't speak for us both, but my reaction was further indifference and despair because it was evident that she had checked out.

Marriage changes the perspective of *"unto the Lord."* Being single in ministry allows you to be solely focused on kingdom building with nothing else to weigh in the balance. Marriage puts a person who has feelings and destiny, not necessarily in front of your purpose, but for sure in the bigger picture. It forces you to be more aware and selfless to even out the things of the Lord in your life because if you neglect what He has put in front of you, your wife, and place career or ministry in the place of her, you've idolized your own path over your union. More importantly, you idolized the promise over the promise giver. How quickly I found myself there.

More importantly, you idolized the promise over the promise giver.

The more and more she pulled away, the less and less I wanted to pull her into it. I was seeing true breakthroughs for people and I figured that was enough to get someone naturally excited to be in ministry. For her, it wasn't. She was dying on the inside. She wasn't feeling loved or that she was placed high on my importance scale. The longer and longer that feeling crept into her life, the more distant she was becoming.

You see the two parallels here—I was happy, excited, and focused, while she was distanced, hurt, and tired. I got to that shift of not caring because I had felt like I spent the first couple of years of dating and marriage trying to get her on board with the "mission-first" mentality because my viewpoint of Christian pastors and leaders seemed to me that they lived a separate life outside of ministry. I had made an idol of effectiveness. I took the Gospel and put it before the biggest ministry He ever gave me, marriage.

My perspective was formed by watching Christian leaders split their personal life and ministry work. The Bible says to walk worthy of the calling with which you were called. I knew I had a great call over my life to do great and mighty things and I couldn't help but wrestle constantly when I would navigate away from being apart from Jesus or ministry. It was a difficult time because I assumed I laid that foundation down but out of fear, I allowed everything else that made us "happy" to be the foundation rather than going after a life with Jesus. I am also not condemning pastors' life choices, but I had a tugging on my heart that my life would consist of truly being sold out to the Gospel. I was so skewed at the time; I was literally willing to do anything to make everything work the way I wanted it.

I can speak to the difference in these life experiences now because I have seen successful marriages that live out "the mission" and have seen their relationships flourish in a time where it was taboo to be all sold out - even if it meant a sacrifice of some privacy or even the risk of losing their loved one to "the call." When I say a risk of losing their loved one, I mean "martyrdom," not divorce. It can be done and I believe it with all my heart. I see the possibility and influence God wants to give unions that look at things of the world and say, *Nah your kingdom is better.*

I couldn't be the type of Christian to clock out of "the call" because I had something else in my life. Honestly, I went about that in a truly misconstrued way. Since then, the Lord has brought me to a correct alignment of how to live according to the Word of God. He has not only re-defined my perspective on marriage, but He also has allowed me to see biblically, the mistakes I made in my pursuit of Him.

In the book of Matthew, Jesus, in two different accounts, talks about the Kingdom of Heaven and refers to a statement that has marked my view of both ministry and marriage. He simply used these choice phrases that sent me into a search of God's way of understanding this specific topic. He said the last who would be first, and the least would be the greatest in the Kingdom (Matt 19:30).

I mentioned earlier that I made being effective in ministry an idol. I believed the lie that if I wasn't doing "something" for God, I was failing. This came from a place of feeling like I was disconnected from a God who is often represented as a loving Father. I saw Him as a Master needing servants, rather than a Dad wanting sons/daughters. A servant is not what He calls me. He calls me a son, and if I didn't do a single thing for the rest of my life in ministry, but instead, became a great husband and great father, He would smile at me and say, *"Son, I am well pleased with you."* I didn't see or think about it then. Because I placed my wife second, I separated my marriage and my ministry.

I saw Him as a Master needing servants, rather than a Dad wanting sons/daughters.

Obviously, a wife comes second to God, but not the things of God. I should have made my relationship with God be what edified her and pulled her closer to wanting to know Him more. I had the lingo of relationship but lived in the outhouse where other Christian servants lived. Instead, I should have known I was a son and could dine on the inside with my Father. This orphan-servant mentality meant that I lived in direct contrast to what God wanted for my life. God was wanting to lead me into an understanding that I was His son and I could do nothing apart from Him, and He wanted nothing of me but to enjoy Him being my Abba (daddy). Instead, I saw Him as a master; and decided to tell Him, *"Don't worry, I'll make you proud of me, watch me work."*

The Gospel of Matthew shows us that when Jesus was baptized, a thunderous voice from heaven said, *"This is my beloved Son, in whom I'm well pleased"*

Matt 3:17. God was pleased with Jesus, way before He even started His public ministry because He had ALWAYS been His Son. And He wants us to receive that same understanding of His love and acceptance of us without needing to work for Him.

Paul understood this. He knew he had persecuted the Christian church much before Jesus encountered him on the road to Damascus. He knew mercy and grace had been extended to his life. Because he knew these things, he set forth to work with God from a place of gratefulness of even being considered worthy to be His son/servant. So, Paul did two great things for all Christians. He showed us that no person is too far away from the love of the Father and that once we receive that love and grace, it doesn't give us the recliner seat, as Corey Russell would say, but it gives us the gratefulness to even be put to work IF He wants to use us.

December 2018 was the start of the downward hill that leads to the heart of this book. It was my birthday weekend and I was in mission mode with my birthday activities. I had my friends make prayer signs and we went out to a major roadway and did drive-thru prayer. It was a blast getting people to pull over and we pray over their requests because this was a town full of people that never saw Christians doing anything like that. Since my little brother's birthday is a week apart from mine, I drove up to my father's house to spend the weekend with them, and unfortunately, my wife couldn't make it.

Getting back from that trip, I was welcomed home with the exciting news that I had an interview with a prospective new bank that could launch my career and change my financial situation for the better. December was looking good.

Monday morning, I had a check-in call with my co-pastor for my young adults' group, because I knew he and his wife were going through some marital issues of their own and I knew we needed to chat about it. He shared that he had a series of conversations with his wife over the weekend that resolved the issues they were facing. I was overjoyed because similarly, my wife and I resolved the same issues that weekend. December seemed to hold a promise of good things to come.

The following day, I got an impression to call him but chose not to. I knew

34

I would give him a call the next day about my interview. He was the person pulling for better job opportunities for me; if an opportunity went well, he was the first to know. After my interview, I immediately called him, but the conversation took a turn very quickly as I sensed he was really troubled on the phone.

I paused to find my words and asked him, "Bro, what's going on?"

He started to weep on the phone, stammering to reply, *"I did it bro...*

"I cheated on my wife."

He continued to apologize to me and the ministry for his failure and his weakness to the lust he had succumbed to. He seemed extremely regretful for the whole thing, to which I did what any pastor buddy would do at the moment - console him the best I could.

Right before he was about to get off the phone, I felt I needed to ask another important question.

"I need to know, did you cheat with someone in the ministry?"

I asked the question to prepare the lead pastor, and if needed, our young adults. He started to weep again and told me he could not say anything at the moment, but that I would find out soon. We prayed and I hung up the phone and quickly called another man that assisted in the ministry.

Getting on the phone with him, our conversation was quick and to the point. Asking if he had heard the news concerning the co-pastor, he replied he did and that he was praying over their marriage and the situation to see the Lord move in the way He needed.

As I was driving home from the interview, I recall the final thing I said to the young man I was on the phone with before hanging up.

"Bro, I don't know why, but I feel like my wife is next."

He remained silent on the phone and with a heavy sigh, his response was a simple *"I hope not."* Pulling into my driveway and walking up to my stairs, I was not prepared for what was about to happen next.

I was met by my wife, my co-pastor's wife, and another young woman in the ministry where they both were consoling her over the news. Apparently, his wife drove straight to our house (which is an hour away), not knowing how else to cope with what was going down. I walked straight in and put my ministering hat on. I knelt down next to her, to let her know things could be restored. I glanced over at my TV and saw they had the movie *War Room* up, ready to be rented, which was another good sign. For those of you that don't know, *War Room* is a really great movie on redemption and fighting for the sanity of your marriage. His wife was visibly torn up about the whole situation.

When I walked in, her weeping was uncontrollable. This was something I rarely saw from her because she was always so easy-going and bubbly. A few minutes into the conversation with her, even though it was one-sided, my wife looked at me and asked if I knew all of what was going on. I told her, *"Yes,"* that I had got off the phone with the co-pastor and moved back to ministering to his wife. His wife decided it was best for her to face her husband; and walked away to get washed up - where I was able to take a quick breather. My wife turned to me on the couch and looked at me and told me she didn't really think I knew what was going on.

The next words out her mouth sobered me to a gripping halt, *"It was with me..."*

I paused and didn't fully understand what she had stated. I looked at her with a stare I've never used before.

She stated again, *"The affair was with me..."*

My initial response was to get up from the couch and stay silent as I walked down to my car and grabbed the tacos I bought from Taco Bell so I could eat.

I walked back up to my dining room table, sat down, and started to eat my meal while the girls proceeded to leave the house. I had no idea why I did any of that, but it was literally my first reaction to the news.

The plan for the day before all this went down was a men's night and women's night for the young adult's group. After the girls left the house, my wife entered the dining room and brought that topic up first. She asked if we should cancel the plans for the night, and I blurted out a big *"No"* because I knew I needed to be around my men. She proceeded to plead that we should have a conversation about the situation, but I didn't have words to say. She began expressing how the affair made her realize how much she loved me and that it was a one-time thing that would never happen again.

My response was as cold as her statement of regret.

> *"If this is what it took for you to realize how much you love me, I don't know what it will take for you to realize how much you need God."*

It was quickly followed by a statement that even left me silent afterward; it still stings till today. She pleaded with me about doing something immediately to start mending the marriage and stated that this situation would prompt an amazing testimony to the goodness of God.

> I cut her off and I said, *"At this point, I'm more concerned with your salvation than our marriage. I would rather shake your hand in heaven than to kiss you goodbye on earth knowing you're going to hell."*

Obviously, I was holding in some deep anger and made an incorrect statement regarding salvation.

At that moment, she left to get to the woman's night. That night, I told my men in that group that I was officially stepping down from any leadership and involvement in the church. I would be taking time to reflect on my relationship with the Lord. We then watched a sermon by Todd White that night - weeping and laughing through the whole message. It was indeed a night I needed.

The following day at work was terrible. I was checked out, as you could imagine. My managers at the time didn't know how to cope with something this severe, so, it made matters worse. My pastor phoned me the following day and asked what I needed. I don't know why I responded with this, but I felt an urge to be alone. I felt the need to get away. Typically, my default reaction to abuse was to run away, but this time it didn't feel like I was running away from something rather than running toward something. I couldn't explain it then, but now I can.

I wound up getting through the rest of the workweek and set up a stay at an Airbnb that weekend. My pastor agreed getting some time alone would be best at this moment. I wanted to honor my wife the best I could in the only way I knew how, so I left the car for her so she could still get to work and do the things she needed to do while I went away. My reason was that during our engagement, her car was totaled - to which I gave her the explanation of not needing two vehicles because we were eventually going to marry and would not need both cars, nor two payments. Something in me, deep down, knew, regardless of getting "caught" in the act of adultery, I couldn't leave her stranded. I wasn't off any hook either. I had still lusted after women, watched pornography, and allowed women in my life emotionally to fill voids that she couldn't. Some would call it shame—I call it having a warm beating heart in the coldness of the hour. It strangely led me to have compassion not from guilt, but from the place of knowing I wasn't perfect either and she still is a person.

Some will call it shame - I call it having a warm beating heart in the coldness of the hour.

My friend Moses (which might be one of the few names I mention in this book), offered to pick me up and take me where I needed to go to be alone that weekend. He didn't know what exactly was going on but knew I needed a friend. I didn't actually tell him the story until about a week later. Honestly, the first night was terrible, which made me doubt that I was doing the right thing. The Airbnb stay was horrendous, to say the least. I couldn't sleep - it just wasn't right. I remember it being a Friday night and I canceled the rest of the trip because it was unbearable. I had another friend pick me up the following morning so I could figure out what to do next.

A friend from the church found the news out that night and called to find out how I was doing. I mentioned I needed to get away and thankfully they had left their home to visit family in another state for Christmas, so they offered for me to stay at their house during that time. The conversations with my wife during that time were minimal. I understood that she didn't appreciate my sudden urge to leave, instead of me wanting to tackle the issue head-on. She was ready to "work" on the relationship, and I was battling whether or not it was worth it. The first night at the house was comforting. My friend, though thousands of miles away, stayed up between calls and texts making sure everything was ok and I was doing better at the moment. It was in a quiet part of town and without having a car and access to people around me, it was nice to just have the word of God, worship, and a place to do it all alone.

An issue I had growing up was that having a friend to count on was my safe zone. I really needed to find comfort all by myself instead of having to rely on another person for it. I preface with that statement because an area that could be viewed from the place of compromise was the conversations with my friend that lent me the house. They, in fact, were harmless in intent, but it could have always been taken incorrectly because of the time of day we spoke, and the consistency of the conversation throughout the day. I bring this small piece of information up not just to give you the whole story but to show even those who might want to slander that I add this to leave no stone unturned. Again, this is not a book to give you facts about an incident but my personal pursuit to seeing whether God was real or if Christianity was another made-up religion. So even in my pursuit, I can always tell you the full truth with nothing to hide and nothing to prove. Little did I know after my first day of house-sitting, everything for me was about to change through a simple music video and an unexplainable encounter with God.

5

The Walk Through Muddy Waters

The second night I was at home, I finally figured out how to work the TV to play some worship music. You all remember I told you that one song I had been introduced to by Upper Room Worship called *Surrounded*. Well, I wound up playing that song again, and knelt down on the floor singing and praying, really not knowing what else to do. Normally, after a song finishes, I stop YouTube and pick another song. That night I got lost in the moment and let the next song play. What played next changed everything that night.

As the song started playing, I couldn't bring myself to change it, even though I had never heard it before. A few seconds into the song, I found myself lost inside the lyrics, especially the bridge:

> *"When I thought I lost me, you knew where I left me, you reintroduced me, to your love. You picked up all my pieces, put me back together, you are the defender, of my heart." Defender- Upper Room (Original by Rita Springer).*

It was as if every stage of the Kubler-Ross grief model hit my heart at that moment. I wept uncontrollably and moved from the denial phase to the acceptance phase within the last 5 minutes of that song. As soon as the song ended, silence hit the room. Nothing else played, and I felt in my heart, words come from a place outside my mind.

The words were clear, *"Let me write the rest of your story, and forgive them."*

This moment was profound because I had spent all those days leading up to this moment, trying to figure out this whole plan for my life. Cycling through my mind were my options of figuring out if I wanted to stay, fight for the marriage, and continue in my Christian walk. I mean, in all honesty, I was ready to throw in the towel with everything. I had tried out this Christian thing and it failed me —so I perceived it at the time. I trusted the system, the people, and the guidance of the church and it seemed no different than the world so what was the point of continuing. So, to hear those words in the darkness of the moment spoke so deeply to the torment in my mind.

There's such a beauty to this piece of the story as I write it. Not just because of the moment but also because of my life since then —how God is into every detail of our lives. When He told me He would write it, it meant to trust Him that if He had the pen it would be an amazing story no matter how it ended up. There is both a trust and a relief that comes when we allow God to lead. I could have taken those words and done my own thing, but I really wanted to see what He wanted to do. I include this because God wants to also write your story.

There is both a trust and a relief that comes when we allow God to lead.

You have commonly heard the saying *"Jesus take the wheel"* and it usually is in reference to a situation we can no longer handle so we ask God to intervene. Him, being a merciful God, will do all that He wills. But imagine a life that didn't constantly need to get to this place. Rather than us choosing our paths, making our own decisions, striving to make things better on our own, we find the peace of what trusting in the God of the Universe, that created you before you even became a physical being, looks like. Let's trust that kind of God again with our life because I can give my own stamp of approval that He is the best writer of the story. I wiped my tears off my face, picked myself up off the floor, and smiled for the first time in a full week.

Minutes after the song ended, I received a text message from my co-pastor's wife. It was a picture of an album cover. It was the same song I had listened to. Ironically, we both wound up listening to the same song, on the same night, at the same time. She felt in her heart to send that to me as an encouragement to lift up our spirits because God had used that song for both of us miles apart. Though we were not communicating, He was speaking directly to us both. It felt as if I had been given a fresh perspective of the situation.

I spent Christmas morning there alone, but it wasn't lonely. For the first time, I felt connected in a way I never had before to the God I spoke so often about. Until that point in time in my Christian walk, I had never been introduced to the reality that He can actually speak to us.

We (Christians) speak about God being alive, but my introduction to Christianity was more about understanding things about Him than having an intimate relationship with Him. The idea of being close to Him didn't seem possible. It was more of a distant relationship from a Father who wrote down dying love letters but never said them to you in person.

The lens you view God with has a direct connection to the way you might have viewed your parents or past relationships with people who had a significant role in your life. I can tell you it's a huge backward approach—because a healthy way of living is to first view God through the lens He has given you to see Him. Then you take that lens and build relationships off that perspective. It works amazingly.

I viewed Him as being distant because I was often emotionally distant from my earthly father. I knew my father loved me, but didn't hear it so much with a tender heart, so why would I expect to hear things like that from God?

Take a moment to ask yourself how you see God. Then take another moment and point back to your relationship with a close relative. Can you see the correlation?

I know I could. I promise, there's freedom in releasing that mentality of God. But trust me, when you have a jaded view of God, it makes your interactions and even Bible reading jaded as well.

I returned home Christmas night, believing in my heart that I was prepared to go from running to working on the marriage. I couldn't provide concrete solutions or definitive answers to what the end road would look like but I was willing to work on it.

From Christmas to New Year's, we tried to process and deal with the reality of what happened, but also navigate through healing together— which, from the perspective of counselors we sought upon during that time, was the best way towards reconciliation. New Year's Eve was the spiral of any progress we thought we gained. I recall her working late that night at the restaurant she waitressed at, and she was really upset at how late she got out. She was also mildly offended at the fact that the young adults of our church all had a planned event where the other couple involved in the affair were both attending, and she felt as if we were cast out of the group.

I explained to her that regardless of our position and current positive work on our marriage, I did not want to engage with the church at that time and felt it was best for us anyway not to be there. In hopes of making things better, I went out and purchased her favorite bottle of champagne. I presented it on our kitchen table with some glasses when she got off work and we went to our patio in the community center, sat down, and celebrated the new year. What I didn't realize was that my tolerance for alcohol was very low, and my decision-making at that time wasn't the best.

For a very strange reason, I now understand this needed to happen. I asked my wife to share with me exactly what happened the day everything unfolded. I felt it best if I knew everything so that the enemy couldn't use hidden information to hurt me later on. She began to explain the incident, and I couldn't bear to hear the rest of the story—which led us to argue and fight, eventually leading us right back to square one.

From that fight, our marriage went right back to a place of tolerance. I almost grew numb once again. I kept pushing to grow awareness about the situation and the restoration of the marriage but had an arm extended out to keep my distance. It took 10 days for something to break open, but it wasn't the breakthrough we both had been pushing for. It was a situation that truly sent us both on a path that neither one of us individually knew where it would end up.

January 10th, 2019 was a day that left a big impact on my life. It was pretty much a typical day for me as it started. My wife and I had been planning to take a retreat up to Atlanta during M.L.K. weekend as we knew we needed to get away, but also have an opportunity to do a heavy three-day intensive counseling session with pastors from Georgia that were walking us through that time. I had been talking to her about really selling everything we owned and moving up there in hopes to save the marriage at that point. I couldn't guarantee her that I was ready to fully commit to staying in the marriage, but I knew I was willing to try anything with action. All those plans had really transpired from the 1st to the 10th, but something drastic shifted that day when I returned home from work.

My good friend was sitting outside my house and I could sense he was not having a good day. By the look on his face, something he was facing at that moment was weighing him down, something heavy. I greeted him, walked him upstairs to my house, and started cooking him some dinner. After our meal, what he was burdened to say he finally felt ready to release.

Now before I say it, I want to add one thing. Truth and honesty become extremely hard when married couples stop being friends. The enemy does a great job at falsely graduating humans that start off as good friends and push them into a title of a spouse, which then undermines all the transparency you both had at the friendship stage. Our desires do oftentimes manipulate friendships into the realm of dating. But what if we didn't have to look at the opposite sex and wonder if they're the one? What if when the Lord shows us who our spouse is and we get into union with them, that we don't lose the friendship in the pursuit of the title of a spouse?

I'm reciting this to you all because that was my whole life—reading deeper than I should have into things that were meant to be platonic and pure, and always trying harder than I needed to make things happen for me. I was losing what was first foundational to my marriage—friendship. With God, all things are possible, and they don't require much of your involvement because He doesn't need you—He wants you. If He needed you He wouldn't be worthy of your worship. He works even when you aren't, He works even when you don't see it.

If He needed you He wouldn't be worthy of your worship.

Best friends share almost everything with each other. Dreams and exciting news are always shared first with them. You trust that this person both can correct you and stand with you in believing for more. I am writing this right now because I know the Lord wants to remind you of this principle. Kingdom friendship doesn't end because you get married—it only enhances intimacy in the friendship.

If you're currently married or single while reading this, I want to pause and say a prayer over this very thing. I believe the Lord will use this testimony and the testimonies of many others in this age to show the world the importance of best friend unions. He is asking us, as believers, to show the world what Kingdom marriage and Kingdom friendship look like. I am led to believe that the relationships I keep and nourish here on earth will ultimately have some resemblance in heaven when we both get there.

There's a very important fact I want to use to give my point: Jesus did return to his disciples to engage in fellowship with them back on earth again after His death and resurrection. While I may not ever be married in heaven, (to whoever she may be), I believe the friendship we cultivated and nurtured here on earth will reap blessings in heaven. All the beautiful memories of friendships here on earth will bring me more joy once I'm reunited with my Savior and those I've run the race well with.

So, let us pause and invite Holy Spirit into this time. Allow Him to show you all the wonderful memories of friendship you have had with your spouse or even friendship with Him. May Holy Spirit prompt you to re-date your spouse and ignite the passion you both had during friendship. I am not talking about a passion for intimacy, but a passion to be all that you can be for that other person. May the dwelling of His presence in your marriage or single life be as the days He walked with Adam in the garden—in full-on communion.

"Lord, bring them back into a first love friendship so they both can commune with You. And for singles reading this book, May the

Lord unloose the anxiety and anticipation of marriage off of you now. May you find the fruit and joy in your singleness. May you recognize the significance of knowing it was "worth the wait". I pray that if you are dating now, that you never leave the realm of Kingdom, godly friendship. That you remain steadfast in the pursuit of protecting that bond that brought you both together in the first place. Thank you, God, for revealing your glory in the unions you have for us. Thank you, God, for manifesting your love for us in the single seasons of our lives, whether they be lifelong or temporary. May no one ever consider a relationship with You to not be enough for their life, in Jesus' name. Amen."

As we sat down, my friend proceeded to talk to me about something that he felt he knew wasn't shared with me back in December, something that he knew my wife could have come to me about in the 3 weeks that led up to this moment. This man was a close friend of our marriage and had no reason to hold his convictions back. He had spent lots of time with my wife as her personal trainer while I was at work since our schedules were opposite each other.

He began by informing me that the beginning of her tunnel season had actually started in November, possibly a month before anything happened with my co-pastor. She had already been more open with her life socially. He also informed me that though it was only one time that she physically interacted with him, the thoughts started way before.

There was even a group code when they would discuss situations not meant for my ears or his wife's ears to know about. They called it the *"Triangle of Trust,"* which I'm glad he broke. I thanked him for being honest with me and apologizing for his failure to come to me sooner. I quickly hugged him and reminded him that it took a true man to come into my home and share all he shared that day. So I fed him some food and sent him on his way while I awaited my wife who did not know I knew the information I was just informed of.

When she got home that night, I asked her if she felt there was anything I needed to know before we went to the retreat we were planning. She didn't mention anything. While getting into bed that night, I prompted her with the information my friend had given me earlier that day, right before we turned off the lights. After explaining in detail everything I had heard, the look on her face said it all. I saw the guilt come crashing over her.

I realized two things at that moment. One, she might have been ready to go the rest of our marriage believing she would have never needed to share that information with me. And two, she had not prepared herself mentally with the thought that I would find out before she had a chance to tell me. Understand that is speculation and assumption, but I knew the feeling of hiding information to try and make things right. I've been that person in the past.

That night, I let her know I would be sleeping in the guest room. My thoughts tormented me through the night. I no longer had a foundation to rely on anymore. I was torn, mad, and numb. I tried my hardest to sleep, but I truly couldn't. My life was so deeply rooted in the relationships I had built and not rooted in Jesus that the crossroad of realizing the true flaw in humanity shook the very core of why I had faith in people in the first place.

The next morning after getting to work, I had taken up an offer to stay at my friend's house during this time and let my wife know that I would be moving out to get some space in light of all that I had found out. My choice to leave wasn't a choice to stop trying to seek restoration and I want that to be clear. I stepped out of the house and created the space to clear out the noise in my own mind.

The Bible says to listen to the whispers of His voice. We must often find a way to remove ourselves from even good things that can deceive the heart in order to hear the Lord clearly on what He is trying to speak over our lives. It's a solemn place of solitude, not isolation. Don't mistake the two. Solitude is knowing and intending to set aside time and space to reflect and muse (meditate) on the Lord and His voice to gain perspective and clarity that you can't have around people.

Webster's dictionary defines amuse as the following: *to divert the attention of so as to deceive.* We have lost the essence of musing with God. Instead of musing, we run after amusement from parks to Netflix and everything in between. We have been gluttons of amusement because rather than sitting in "it"—whatever it may be for your life, we run to distract or deceive our brains into thinking that if we just hang away long enough the problem might just go away on its own. We often just zone out because the problem is just "too much to handle." I encourage you to read Psalms 77 on your downtime. I love this piece of scripture because it talks simply about what David did to handle his hard situations and how we today respond so differently to them now. We find ourselves distanced from the issues in life in hopes that they kind of fade away rather than considering David's two keys to resolution.

The first is remembrance. We forget all the good that has been done in our lives and see the situation from such a large position that it often makes us outweigh the good. Secondly, we chose to amuse than muse. Silencing the noise of the world and reading His word is not the first practice most people go to for answers. Rather than focusing on Him and consecrating ourselves, we choose to detach, choose to engage in meaningless things, or worse—we choose to isolate. Isolation is blinking and realizing time has passed by and you've cut people off—cut off engaging in society, and cut off the fellowship of Jesus. We choose not to go after what He is saying to us and choose not to fight, not to contend, and allow outside voices to speak against situations in our lives.

Around the time I was getting my things out of the house and heading to my friend's house, the church I attended started a 21-day Daniel fast (which was my first ever fast honorably), and my friend and I decided to take the fast on, full steam. We did this not only to benefit (honestly) our spirits but also our bodies. *Losing 35lbs in 3 weeks probably wasn't the healthiest, but gosh, it worked.*

Embarking on the fasting journey meant one thing for me—clarity. At the beginning of the fast, up to that point in my relationship with God, I had only one encounter with the Father around the incident. You remember, *"Let me write your story?"* I understood the basics of fasting but still had no idea about the spiritual implications that fasting brought when I let go of the things my body wanted. In other words, I had no instruction on what would actually happen if I let go of what I wanted and let Him do His work. So, I decided to submit a request to Him which was simply *"Lord, do I stay or walk away?"*

This was a simple question that would hopefully have a simple answer even though I had no idea how I would get it. To better explain the significance of this fast, let me elaborate on what fasting is. It is intentionally denying the things that brought me joy in life in order to gain a response from the Holy Spirit because I was giving God the first position, or rather removing what I placed there before Him. It means renouncing the natural in order to invoke the supernatural.

To put it simply, I was coming into alignment with what my spirit was trying to uncover for me from God. You may think it sounds backward but the Bible often shows us how when in our weakness (physically) it is the pristine opportunity for the Lord to work on our behalf. He flexes when we can't. It's a beautiful display of how wonderful and mighty God is and how He truly reigns overall.

If you've never tried fasting before, I implore you to do it. Start slow, maybe once a week and you choose the day; work your way up to committing to a consecrated time period with God. He gets excited to see hearts come alive during a fast. When you do it, don't do it with the thought, *"oh if I fast, He will give me something."* No, that's not the way it works. He already gave you everything you needed on the cross.

A fast is giving your body a reminder that it can be weak and taking that which you desire and putting it under the direction of God to show Him you faithfully agree that He is indeed the author and finisher of our faith, that He is supreme being overall, and that you—the created special one of His very breath—would be willing to yield to His direction.

Looking back, the beauty of doing that fast at that time was that I didn't have much distraction. I can tell you that I didn't get extra spiritual, meaning I don't recall praying any more than I usually did, or reading the Word any more than I would on a normal basis. But the Lord met me during that fast, solely because I was allowing myself to come to the surface and to be exposed to the Son. It was a true John 15 (God as the Vine Keeper) moment for me. It's a beautiful display of God and His tending to us as branches attached to the vine (Him). It was a time where the Lord lifted me up to expose me to the sun and pruned away the excess, in order for me to grow. My friend and I trained our bodies; and somehow, the Lord used that training to prepare me for what He was bringing to the surface in the spirit a few weeks later.

While I rejoiced in a huge physical transition, the Lord was working out the details in the spirit saying, *"I am carving a path for you son, to get to a place to hear me."*

I'll use this analogy: I was 35 lbs. over-weight; which meant I had "extra fat." In the training, my body started to release toxins and fat while I ate right and worked out my body. The physical changes started to show as a result of putting in hard work. When the Lord sees that you are willing to remove the excess, it gives Him access to start to unveil your spirit to align with your "sacrifice" in fasting so you can hear, see, and feel Him more clearly. It's similar to the way you'll see muscle more clearly when the fat goes away - the Lord is able to surface Himself when the excess is put away.

To be clear, I'm not saying you HAVE to fast in order to hear or receive from Him, but oftentimes big transitions and needing clarity both require cleansing even in the natural, call it a spiritual laxative.

After about two and a half weeks of the fast, my dear friend Moses invited me to a young adult's event at a local church. I hadn't really been to church in a while and my weekends looked nothing like they used to. It was a Friday night, and I would have probably spent it right at home, so reluctantly I said, "yes" to go.

He told me it started at 7:00 PM and I told him I would meet him there. I showed up right at 7:00 PM on the dot alone, because my friend joined me an hour later because he is that kind of friend that loves making an entrance. I was excited to go although, as the time crept closer because I knew that no one there would know me, and I wouldn't know them. I could worship and listen without any distraction or judgment. When I got there, the band began playing and I was really caught by surprise. For the first time in my Christian walk, I was in a service where worship through song went on longer than 30 minutes.

I remember even looking at my watch thinking *Wow, we're at an hour? It probably only gets better from here!* As I sat in the front row of that church, the sermon started. The pastor preached on Spiritual Warfare—something I was not very familiar with at the time, but I said to myself, *Hey, I'm here for a reason, let's dive in.* After the sermon ended, they went back into worship, which again was so sweet to me.

While the worship band was finishing up the set, and I was worshipping the Lord on my own, a man came up to me from the band and said that the Lord had a word for me. Now to the spirit-filled Christian reader, you may understand where this is going. But let me remind you of one thing - up until this point I literally had no clue what this meant.

I feel the urge to reiterate that because everything that follows this sentence has both truth and a witness to it, remember Moses being at the church. I feel led to explain more about this term to help better align even those that don't know, with what happens next.

A "word" simply put is an unction from God that we as sons/daughters of God know so surely that God wants to say something specific to that person or persons in front of us. This word biblically can be attributed to something called prophecy or words of knowledge—both having a wonderful set of unique characteristics that one can easily define the two.

A word of knowledge is a specific statement that God gives someone to provide insight into something important to the person receiving the information (that was never shared previously with the person giving the word) in order to help align the recipient with the reality that God knows their story/ their life and that He speaks to His children regularly.

The latter which is prophecy or prophetic words are used to both remind the recipient of things that person has been believing for or praying for and also exhorting (encouraging) that person into a higher level of belief and faith for promises that God has spoken to them about to continue on the path they are going. *I hope this brief 101 Intro to Spiritual Gifts brought to you by Derek Diaz was informative enough. Back to our regularly scheduled programming.*

As this man from that church stood in front of me, he looked me in the eye and said, *"The Lord wants you to know that you're exactly*

WHY DID I GET SAVED?

where you're supposed to be and doing exactly what you're supposed to be doing."

I said, *"Amen."*

He paused and looked at me again and said, *"I also saw a vision of you. It was as if you were floating in the middle of the sea on an inner tube all alone on the ocean. But as the Lord brought my vision higher, I could tell that you were simply drifting in the palms of His hands, and the ocean was actually a very small pond in His hands."*

I must note here that this man did not know anything about me, nor knew the situation. He began to tell me he had one more word for me, but he wanted to make sure that the word came from the Lord, and he politely asked if I minded if he could pray in tongues. Up until this point in my faith, I had never heard of tongues, so I shrugged my shoulders and said, *"Sure, why not!"*

Don't lose me here family, I want to explain tongues briefly as well now because all of this was new to me at that point in my life as well.

Tongues as described in the book of Acts and explained by the Apostle Paul are a language designed for heaven. An utterance that often bubbles up from the belly where words collide that don't often resemble any language at all (sometimes). These words are used specifically to communicate with heaven and God.

The Apostle Paul states in 1 Corinthians 14:2;14-15, the importance and direction tongues give the body of Christ. If you feel as if you have never experienced tongues, I urge you to study Paul and the Apostle's journeys post-Jesus when he delivered them the gift of Holy Spirit as He promised while He was alive. After studying, pray. Pray that He helps you see you've been given the same spirit He gave the early church, pray He bubbles in you the same utterances the disciples had all those years ago. If those utterances don't come it doesn't disqualify you from the Holy Spirit. Much like myself I again remind you that none of this was ever spoken or explained to me most of it just happened. If you're asking why, all I can describe it as was that this was my Jeremiah 29:13 time in my life. I sought Him wholeheartedly and was promised I would find him and this time, not to understand Him but know Him.

As he prayed in tongues, I felt holy respect at the moment - like this guy really wanted to make sure this was not him. With my friend standing as my witness, the man stopped praying in tongues and looked me in the eyes with tears on his face.

"The Lord wants you to know it's ok, it's ok to walk away."

I lost it. I wept together with him on the carpet for 15 minutes before I could even muster up the courage to tell him what that meant to me.

I want to break down the words, so you have a clearer picture.

1. Being exactly where I was supposed to be and doing exactly what I was supposed to do: I interpreted that word as making the decision to fast and separate myself from the home to allow the Lord to have His way over my life. This was a big step in the process of the whole ordeal. It went against the advice of most people but is ultimately what gave the Lord the most freedom to move in my life.

2. The vision: You may have wondered why the cover of the book looked this way. Well, what you didn't know was how much loneliness I felt in that season. It was as if I felt that everyone had so many opposing opinions about the situation that I honestly felt I couldn't rely on anyone but God, to help give me clarity and guidance on the matter. So, floating alone was the feeling I had though having all the friends in the world, pastors, worshipers, evangelists, but no one could really be there for me. This topic alone is a difficult one for the church.

3. The final word: Well, what can I say. In the book of Judges, Gideon (to note a timid doubter) put out a request to the Lord and asked for a miraculous sign to know what the Lord had said was indeed coming

to pass. Asking the Lord that question, "Do I stay or walk away?" was my only request. When the man first asked to pray in tongues (Paul in 1 Corinthians 14:2 when a man prays in tongues he doesn't speak to men but to God), I knew he was submitting to God on the unction he had gotten from the Lord, to speak the word and was literally double-checking to make sure it was God and not his own imagination. Then, for him to precisely and accurately give the word back to me exactly the way I had asked God, was a sure sign the Lord was on it. It also was preparing me for something I truly wouldn't have been ready for a few days later.

This whole experience opened up a way for the Lord to work on my character and heart in a way no one person could have ever done in that season. It gave me unknown confidence that He was greater and bigger than my situation. He would guide me and keep me in peace no matter what the outcome or circumstance.

I now know that character is so important. Reaction especially from the side of our human nature is not the response God intends from us. He gave us our personality and individual humanity so we each have different ways of responding. But our role in the world is not to react, but to set the pace and action on how God's people move during storms. It's why I question how people say they're in love with God, but hate the world when the world comes crashing down on them.

John in his epistle notes that if we love God and don't love people then we have no love at all and ultimately don't have God. Consider that, it might sound extreme, but it's His heart, He loves EVERYONE. He also loves through every tough time the world faces. There is not a single person living right now He doesn't love; loving His enemies is one of His greatest accomplishments next to the cross and I'm in constant pursuit of wanting to know how to love as He did.

6

There Is Light Peeking Through

The day after that experience, I had a boldness to step back into everything that I walked away from regarding the church. That encounter with that man was Friday night, and by Saturday, I decided to rejoin my young adult community for the first time since the incident.

When I arrived, I was saddened to find that they really didn't pause to reflect. They tried to push through the situation and continue the book study we started in September. I stepped in and asked them to put the book away and allow the people that were present to share the feelings they may have had since it all went down. Knowing it had been over a month since the incident, it shocked me to know that there wasn't much guidance and support for them.

The reality is that affairs and divorce don't just affect the couple but also the congregation as a whole. Those people had put prayers, faith, and value in that relationship. We often try as a church to keep those incidents under a tight seal in efforts to keep a huge headliner off the Sunday print in the news, failing to help guide also those that may have been close to them, did ministry with them, or sat under them.

One by one, I could tell by the way people were communicating, they hadn't released much of their feelings and were growing cold to the reality of a loving Father who is willing to go there (a deep place) with them in their feelings. A lot of healing took place that night while people got to share where they were. I also shared where I was, along with the co-pastor's wife.

The following day, I attended our church service and it would be the first time I entered that building since the incident. A wave of different emotions hit me while still on the block approaching the building. I remember sitting in my car shaking and trembling in fear and an elder of the church who noticed my car opened my passenger door got inside, sat silently, and just we wept together.

> Turning to me, he said, *"I don't know how you are managing to do this without conflict, but son, I am proud of you, you are showing me that you're a better man than I am."*

Tears continued to fall, and words were exchanged, but once he left, I had to find the confidence to walk into the church knowing I was going headfirst into the reality of my entire situation. I got out of my car and proceeded to walk. As I saw my dear friends at the doors of the building, I started weeping uncontrollably, not being able to get words out. Every person that saw me and walked up to me couldn't do anything but cry with me.

As more and more people noticed my return, I wanted to maintain the dignity of the house so I decided to sit with my wife because she was also attending that Sunday and it was the honorable thing to do. After the service, I walked to the back of the church building to see the children that I had been pastoring over the last year and greet them all. Laughs and tears flooded as we all hugged and said "Hi" and" Bye" as I started to walk back to my car.

While walking, I saw for the first time since December the man who had the affair with my wife. He was speaking to the lead pastor's wife and noticed me out the corner of his eye and tears started streaming down his face.

As I got closer and closer, he hung his head down in shame and disappointment. A sea of different emotions and thoughts ran through my head. The closer I got, I puzzled with the thoughts of what I should do kept flooding my mind. *What do I say?* Finally standing in front of him, all I could think to do was hug him. I gave him a smack on the back of the head similar to what a man would do to another man, playful not aggressive, and simply walked away.

I recall getting into my car, pulling down my visor, and crying with a deep howling cry. The first question that finally came to my mind was, *"why Lord? Why didn't I hit him?"* What a holy question, right? I asked because I had made a reputation back in the day of hitting first, asking questions later. The response that I got has marked my life ever since that day. It was such a sweet response from the Lord.

He gently told my spirit, *"Son, a hug did more damage to the devil, than a punch would have ever done."*

Oh, how that comment continued to pour out tears down my face; finally coming to a place of knowing what it was like for Jesus to stand in front of Judas and receive the kiss of betrayal without a knee-jerk Peter reaction. It's important for me to talk about this interaction from a biblical standpoint to understand who Jesus is in even the toughest of times.

In the Gospel of John, we hear Jesus give a prophetic "secret" to John that He couldn't trust to any other disciple. While John laid his head on Jesus' chest during the last supper, Jesus whispered in his ear the name of the person who would eventually betray Him. I had read those verses over and over through my years and did not see the beauty of the moment because my experiences didn't match the situation until now. I had been more of a Peter in the early stages of my walk, and it's exactly why I couldn't be trusted in situations like the one I was in that day with that man a few years back. John trusted that Jesus knew what He was doing leading up to the cross and Jesus trusted John to know that He had everything in control. There was a trust there that Jesus couldn't give to anyone else in the room which was full of His disciples.

So, I veer a bit off track to remind you all that proximity and intimacy are the keys to receiving His heart on how to handle every situation that may come into your life. Why was it Peter and not John who pulled his sword to cut the soldier's ear? Because prior to the kiss of betrayal, John already had the insight into it happening. He had rested in the promise of his Savior's death and resurrection. This was an understanding that took Peter much longer to obtain because Peter did things "his" own way. Oh, how this helped me in my situation. There was already a promise God wrote over this point of my life.

"Let me write your story" rang over and over again every time I wanted to run, every time I wanted to give up, and every time I wanted to turn my back on everything. I encourage you, no matter where you are, to get close to Him and allow the proximity of His very being to speak words into you on how to handle the situations your life may face. I can attest to His voice being as soft as a whisper but as mighty as a roaring lion in my heart even in the wildest of times. This encouragement only comes from my place of walking this out in my own life. I would not write this to you had I not first done it. Despite my circumstance, I trusted and ironically allowed Jesus to lead me through it.

Whatever your situation, let Him lead you, the Bible tells us that there is a way that seems right to a man, but it ultimately leads to destruction. I know looking back I could have easily led myself into some wayward paths all because I wanted to satisfy myself rather than be still. Allow yourself the grace to do the one thing America really doesn't teach us much to do, wait, and relax.

I wasn't rushing to get answers, and I sure wasn't rushing to get out of anything, every step was led by Him, and in every situation I found myself in He already saw the outcome, which is why He trusted me to go through it. I feel the need to expand on this to help clarify those statements.

We in America have been sold a lie. Grind All Day, Change the World, Chase the Dream, all phrases I can pull out from most of the top best-selling author's books in America on self-confidence, wealth, and success. Imagine those same people releasing a book that said, Rest and Wait, Trust in the Lord, Don't Strive for Position, Take a Hold of His Yolk, I'm sure they wouldn't do as well in the stores that time around. America has been told we must wake up earlier, grind harder, and caffeinate ourselves into early deaths in all to create success and conquering our dreams. I might be going in a different direction in this book but follow me it applies. Just because I got the word about walking away I didn't automatically send out a mass text with the title I'm Single on it. I didn't run off and grab paperwork to start the divorce process. I kept going day by day. Understanding something was going to happen but it was at His timing.

The Bible says in Song of Songs Chapter 2:7, *"That you'll not disturb my love until she is ready to arise."* The Lord gave me insight into this verse of scripture by explaining to me that love awakened (disturbed) before its timing is considered lust to Him. So whether it be to run away from love, start a business, start a relationship, or open a ministry, we must seek His timing first before moving forward. Noting all this I hope you can understand why even in the interaction with the man at my church, rather than just jump to the first reaction of who I was before, I slowed myself down because I trusted Him. He trusts you the same way he trusted John. Will you trust Him?

Had I not had experiences with Him in the days leading up to that Sunday, I would have quite possibly handled that situation at the church much differently and my natural ways could have gotten the better of me. Driving off that day, I felt like I had won a strong battle for the Lord. I felt like somehow even though I didn't understand anything about the Spirit of God, I knew the devil lost that day. What I wasn't prepared for was one of his final attempts to rob me of everything the Lord has been doing in that prior week.

Monday was a pivotal day for me. Starting off pretty similar to any other week, it was led with work and a chiropractic appointment, and some working out. At some point in the middle of my workday, my wife started to franticly call me a number of times; but I couldn't answer because of my clients. I finally was able to reach back out and she was requesting that I come to the house to sit and meet with her that night. I couldn't make that happen because immediately after my workday, I had to get to that chiro appointment. I could sense the urgency in her tone though.

Before we hung up the phone, after I repeatedly told her that I wouldn't be able to meet, her last comment struck a deep chord in my heart. I can hear the words even as I type today. They were subtle; yet powerful. She responded to my *"No"* with a, *"Well, just know I tried to tell you before you found out."*

I hung up the phone and couldn't get my mind off the comment. My doctor called me shortly after to inform me that they pushed my appointment back later that evening, which gave me two hours to spare, to which I let her know that I would be able to come by to hear what she had to say. Somehow the Lord was working it all out in the background all over again. To confess to the feelings that day, anxiety and fear came over me in a way that I hadn't affiliated with for some time. I was dreading it, but I knew He wanted it to happen. I got off work and headed to the house, informing her to open up the garage and place two seats outside so we could talk without having to go into the home. I didn't feel right sitting in the very place the affair happened.

As we sat there, I could see her brokenness for the first time since the whole thing went down. I mean it was the first time seeing her in about three weeks. He truly changed my heart at the moment where I might have been numb and dull, my heart didn't want to leave the garage if there was stuff we needed to work out. She had confessed how hard it had been for her personally to walk through this situation alone, but because sin had wrapped itself around her and gripped her, even friends that were supporting her throughout that time decided it was best to part ways so she truly did not have anyone with her.

It had been over a month since finding out about the affair and about 3 weeks since I had moved out. Throughout those three weeks, we were consistently trying to arrange calls and meetings with pastors helping us in reconciliation. Worthy to note that I decided a few days before that trip to Georgia, that it wasn't best to go. She had mentioned another retreat that her girls brought her to, which happened to fall on the same weekend. I naturally saw it as a divine message that the Lord did not want me to go.

> I'm telling you all this now to give context to the intensity of this moment for both of us because so much did happen in January that as we were nearing the end of the month, it was as if all the moments and emotions got encapsulated in this 2-hour meeting.
>
> To honor her, I will be leaving out details of the conversation, but please note that I will do my best to give you the raw heartfelt moment we shared while sitting in that garage together.

I see the image of the moment clearly. It was the open garage with two chairs sitting in the middle, a combination of our things tossed around our place, still there not touched for the last month. We started to talk and I could hear the timidity in her voice. Something deep was inside of her that she needed to get out.

It started off casual, but once I knew we both were circling around where we needed to go, I asked her to get on track on why she called me earlier that day. I proceeded to ask her if she had mentioned anything to her family because I knew they could provide some support for her that I couldn't and didn't want to provide at the time. She had been silent toward her family during those three weeks and it took a toll on her emotionally.

From that place, I would assume anyone that didn't have support could sink fast. She then proceeded to explain what her past three weeks looked like - how the retreat trip went for her and what not going to Georgia meant for her. After some time explaining, I was also able to explain what happened to me but didn't fill her in about the experience at the other church. When the conversation finally went where it needed to go, it opened up the daunting comment she left earlier in the day, *"I tried to tell you before you found out."*

As we approached her finally revealing what this urgent meeting was for, she instantly started to tear up. In a true confession with sorrow and grief, she began to explain how the man and she had continued in their affair during that time we both took to seek reconciliation. Much of the moments of considered *"breakthrough,"* and moments with women in her life that sacrificed themselves to help her, were really things that couldn't break through the grip of loneliness that fell upon her and lust that fell upon them both. I sat there in silence with disbelief.

I thought back to that word I received that previous Friday night thinking if this really would be the way. Friends, I must tell you I've preached about biblical stories in the Bible such as Hosea and Gomer multiple times. Accounts in the Bible that speak to the heart of God using the prophet Hosea to remarry his wife who walked away from their union and choosing to buy her back at whatever the cost because God loved his people too much to allow them to stay in their sin.

I was caught up believing I had been given divine access to the Lord to hear from Him about my own situation, but truly spent a lot of time doubting

His direction for it and believing if it really came from Him. I was wedged in a crosswind because this decision affects the rest of my life and hers. As I gathered my thoughts, the next words out of my mouth cut thick like a dagger.

"In light of this news, I need to let you know I'll be pursuing a divorce."

A groan came out of her for the first time in the two years of marriage—one that I never heard before. This is the type of scream cry when everything gets caught in your throat and you can't breathe. She knew then I had had enough. This was the day everything broke. I had finally gotten to a place where I knew it was time.

I proceeded to explain through her tears how I would not leave her hanging and would help finish everything we started together, but that I would be getting the rest of my belongings from the apartment and proceeding with the paperwork. I remember encouraging her to seek the Lord as she never had before. I wanted her to use this moment and opportunity to really go after what she believed.

It was all I had left to say. I also reminded her that she was worth His death, and she was smart enough to pick up from this place and continue going. It wasn't that I wanted to be cold. I think I submitted my emotions at that moment to the Lord to allow Him to work on her, instead of feeding into anger or sadness.

With those final words, I got up, gave her a hug, and left the home, and headed to my appointment. That was one of the last few times we really sat down to talk ever again before the final divorce day. My drive to the chiro place was quiet, almost like I wasn't driving or fully present. Everything was just silent.

When I got out of my appointment, my next call was to my lead pastor. I remember talking to him on the drive back to the apartment I was staying at, and as I entered the house, I walked over to a little section of the apartment the man I was living with set aside for my clothes. I broke down weeping and sunk into the floor.

Yelling *"Why me, why did I have to go through this?"*

It was my breaking-point time. At my friend's house, I wept not understanding something about God I know now, this time I was tired, tired of being dealt with these devastating disappointments. On the floor, with the phone laid out to the side, I knew I had been dealt the biggest blow my life had ever seen - and I have been through some stuff. My pastor was left speechless.

Words couldn't mend what was happening internally and we both knew it. At this moment I really didn't know how to seek the Lord, even in the way I was advising her to do it because I was so afraid to be left alone. I know now something I didn't know then—the confidence of knowing He is always with me and He is not ever too far for me to feel His presence. From that call, I had one mission. I needed to get through this Daniel fast, work on myself, and cultivate a new Derek.

The Freedom Contract was birthed in this season. It was a covenant (contract) I made with the Lord to take the next 8 months and be completely sold out to Him in prayer and declaration. I had a dream about it and wrote it out one day at work. It was worded very eloquently and sounded like a legitimate contract to which I even had my friend witness and sign it with me. To this day I keep the original copy to remind me of my dedication in that season.

The enemy still had a grip on areas of my life because I wasn't declaring who I was in Christ over those areas, and prayer was something so inconsistent in me that I continued to allow opinions and other voices to dictate my path. Those times were over for me. From that conversation to about the middle of February, I made sure the devil knew he messed up, big time.

I sought after righteousness and holiness even though I didn't know exactly what it meant. I knew I needed to do it. I immersed myself back into my community. I saw an opportunity to lead and did it from a completely different place. It was a humble place, one that was willing to serve even though I was looked upon as a leader. I lived in the moment and enjoyed time with everyone who was still in my life. If it was a walk down a path or a beach day, I made myself a part of the lives of people that remained so in that we wouldn't feel as if the ship sank everyone.

Around this same time, I was prepping myself and a team of people to join me in going to a day-long conference in Orlando, so that we could see and hear from the two men that really changed my perspective on Christianity, Todd White, and Francis Chan. The conference was called The Send. We took it as a young adult's team trip but didn't really know what to expect. We knew we all wanted to go and be together to experience it.

While planning the trip, a momma and poppa from church the Mansfield's, who had a history in the Brownsville revival back in the '90s, caught wind of what we were doing and what we were planning. After introducing them to Upper Room worship, they knew they needed to be there as well. So, they booked a hotel and planned to travel up to be there with us. It was all set for us to go.

We had a home set up for us from one of the members of the church we were all staying at, the van was rented and ready to go, and the team was all packed and excited to hear from the speakers and worship teams, but what we didn't know was how this experience would change the rest of the course of our lives and lifted the spirits of those who went that day.

7

The Send

I was hungry for God to say the least. I was hungry to know way more about a world of Christianity I felt I was somehow left out of. Upper Room's worship was unlocking a thirst for more. They sang to the Lord in a way I had never heard before. Used words and phrases I never heard worship leaders recite before. It was all so new yet it didn't scare me, it led me to believe this is what loving Him undignified looked like.

Upon finding out that they were going to be attending a pre-conference weekly service, Tom, Kenny, and I decided on a random Wednesday night, right after work, we would drive all the way up to Orlando to try and catch them. It was a 2.5-hour drive to catch 2 hours of worship and then drive back that very night because I had work the next day. We were nothing short of crazy.

Two 20-year-old men and a 60-year-old hopped in one car and took off. When we got to the church, it was as if the Lord himself was shining a light in my face of a world about Himself I had never seen before. Sure, we all had been to conferences before and experienced large arena-style meetings, but it was nothing like what Kenny and I were seeing that night. And to think it was only a taste of the real thing that was about to happen a few days after.

What we saw that night was unbelievable. We watched men and women dance with freedom—both young and old people sing with their hearts full of joy. There were people praying for each other at random that didn't require an alter call or someone on a microphone guiding the herd. It seemed like people knew exactly who they were and operated exactly as they saw fit on how the Lord wanted to move. It was so different, yet it felt so real.

We went, we experienced, we enjoyed, and we turned right back around to head home. A big excitement filled our hearts seeing tangibly for a brief moment what we were about to see on a full scale in a few days.

The next couple of days were like a big blur. I recall requesting to get off work early Friday because I wanted to get on the road as soon as possible to try and get to the same event Friday night to have another taste. When you look back at significant times of your life after much time has settled, it allows you to really tap into the emotions and feelings you had during and leading up to the big changes.

Writing this story out especially this part, I see how I was so unfamiliar with everything that was going on around me, but also equally excited because it felt absolutely right. I must add that I wasn't filling my void of what happened with my wife with something shiny and pretty to redirect my focus. This arena of Christianity was foreign to me. This experience was foreign to me. Being content in Him removes the necessity of finding the next best thing because He is the best thing.

In Him, all things exist and He draws all men near to Him and this was His doing, not mine. It may sound like a rant to justify myself, but because I came from a background of not knowing Jesus and thought like the people who didn't know Jesus, I can easily understand the thoughts of critics because I was once one of them. Even though you have made it this far in the book, you can still look at it and say I placed myself to be emotionally available to look for a replacement to fill the void. I need to you hear these words as I say them *"Jesus is the fulfillment and the answer to any void. He was never absent from the void and waited patiently for me to make Him center, so He could show off and flex all He really was to me."*

Being content in Him removes the necessity of finding the next best thing because He is the best thing.

The journey towards understanding how He really joins Himself to us as the peace that surpasses all understanding, as the Apostle Paul says, doesn't have to be a long and tough one to go on. Actually, Jesus made it quite simple by allowing us to understand that if we gave Him what was never ours to hold on to, He exchanges it for Himself. Who is He?

He is the Prince of Peace and the Deliverer of rest to our soul. All anxiety, and depression, and any discomfort of any situation you may be facing, He simply asks to take it from you so that you may receive Him fully. It's such a beautiful exchange and so simple that people call it too good to be true. But as I write these words out to you now, knowing what I have walked through, you can understand how I can smile and rejoice knowing He fully satisfies my soul and is the direct fulfillment to all of my needs.

He is the Prince of Peace and the Deliverer of rest to our soul.

Kenny and I signed up to be volunteers for the conference which meant we needed to be at the location earlier than most of the people we came with. We felt led to serve at any capacity we could because this was actually a free event. When we arrived on Friday night and got directly to the church, we were met by some friends there who also traveled from West Palm Beach. One of those friends Byron would later become one of the greatest men in my life and I am truly grateful to call him a brother now. To watch as the team of people that came to the event with me got to let go of all that burdened them, and experience that Friday night worship, was simply amazing. Being able to watch them all in their own unique way and be free in worship was worth the whole trip. Again, this was just a taste of what tomorrow was bringing.

The following morning, Kenny and I rose early and took part of the team with us to the stadium for those that wanted to get in line early and get good seats. As we entered Camping World Stadium, a thought came across my mind. Two years prior, I was in the same arena attending Wrestle Mania 33, which was a bucket list goal of mine.

Now I was back in the same stadium that before was completely packed out for a sporting event, but this time I was feeling so much more fulfilled than that time. Both times being at that stadium were honestly the only times in my life I did something for myself. Back then, it was because of what wrestling meant for me, and now because I knew somehow this event would change my life.

As the day started, Kenny and I were given our section to look over and given instructions on what to expect when doors opened and people started entering in. Such a rush of purpose and joy-filled us both as we started to see young people run from the back of the football stadium hurrying to get to the very front of the stage so they could see all the action up close and personal. We were given seat savers for members of our team and were allowed to save specific sections which made our transition after we were done serving, relatively easy.

The first half of the day consisted of Kenny and I greeting, directing, and handing out booklets and flyers on behalf of the conference. It was such a joyous moment for us to selflessly serve something much bigger than ourselves. Worship leader after worship leader, speaker after speaker, we truly were grateful to be there. I personally kept telling myself, *"I barely know anyone coming out to sing or speak, but Lord, you have us here for a reason. Let's get this thing rolling."*

You may be asking why I'm emphasizing this day so much. Well this day, February 23, 2019, will forever be the day I allowed the Lord to truly start the process of setting me free.

In the early afternoon, Kenny and I finished our serving time and by then some of our team had decided to head to the field to get space to move around to worship and dance. As we neared the end of our shift, I remember staying back in the seats we saved to allow our friends to get lunch while I watched over bags and seats.

At some point, while sitting in those seats, I completely forgot about me being there. I remember looking out on the field and seeing thousands of young people like me—hungry, crying, laughing, and something really different, dancing. Now, I don't mean jumping up and down or lifting your hands. I mean contemporary ballet movements. It didn't seem out of place, but I found it so odd to be in the middle of a Christian conference. Yet it was the dancing that captivated me.

Just by watching, something was burning within me. Since my team was already on the field, I decided to leave our seats behind when some came back from lunch. I went down to the field to join Kenny and a few of them down there. It had been some time of enjoying the worship and sitting down to hear some sermons from speakers. There was a call to pray, and we were asked to gather in groups of 4 and start praying for our nation. Kenny and I joined hands with two other people that were near us and started to pray passionate prayers for our great country.

After some more time on the field, there was a section of the conference where pastors from around the nation gathered together to declare and pray over specific regions and issues in the church and in our world, they felt led to pray against. At some point during the day, a young black pastor who I believe was from Chicago gathered the stadium to pray and specifically asked for the majority to pray for minorities. Assuming I'd include myself in the minority, I closed my eyes and stood in position, and started to feel hands circling around me. I hadn't realized how at that moment I was considered a true minority to the people around me.

As all of them started to pray their own individual prayers, I started to feel something... In my belly grew this tingling feeling. Within moments, I began breathing extremely heavily as if I needed to exhale a lot of built-up air. The tingling then spread throughout my body until it was covering the entire surface area of my body. I remember my mind questioning why no one else felt what I was feeling because I clearly opened my eyes and saw their hands were on places that the feeling was coursing through. I couldn't speak to tell them to stop because it had felt so strong it tensed up every muscle in my body.

The intensity of the electricity I felt in my body got so severe it brought me to my knees where they continued to pray for me until they were asked to finish up the prayers by the pastors on the stage. I remember closing my eyes again, still kneeling on the ground and feeling like I couldn't move and completely drained. The electricity was still running through my body and I couldn't bring myself to understand what was happening.

As I was kneeling, an extreme heaviness forced me on my back—completely laid out face up to the sun. The only way I could describe it was my arms were locked in a position that looked similar to what a T-rex would look like and I was stone-cold still for at least 45 minutes to an hour. Not one single movement, I'm sure if I didn't have to blink I wouldn't have done that either. Everyone around me left me there. They all just knew I was experiencing something bigger than them.

I had no idea what was happening to me. After some time, I gained mobility in my left arm again and I remember reaching out to my poppa from the church who was there around us. The moment I grabbed his leg, the electricity shot up my arm and all over my body again. Another full-on blow of this feeling came rushing through my body, and I had to just let it happen again. I eventually got up after another 15 minutes and finally started to move around probably looking to everyone around me like I was drunk.

I was in such a daze for a little while completely stuck in my head, I tried my best to comprehend what happened. When I couldn't even bring myself to any reality of what happened, I decided to give up, sit back, and enjoy the moment I had just had with the Lord even if I didn't know what went down.

When I felt completely better, it was like a fire in me busted open and I started running around to people to pray for them. It was something I was used to doing even from before, but there was a huge difference now. Every prayer I was praying was leaving people in tears and in shock and awe. People would look at me with amazed and stunned faces.

"How did you know that? How are you praying for something I've never told anyone? How did you know I wanted to go to this specific place?"

I couldn't understand why they questioned it. I just kept praying. Sometime in the night, as I was walking around, I noticed someone out of the corner of my eye. It was a friend named David who I knew from my first original church. We locked eyes and ran to each other and embraced and hugged and cried together. The Lord instantly brought me back to a time where he invited me out to experience more of what God had for His children and I remember saying no. That where I was in my walk with God was fine to me. I cried and thanked him for planting that seed so many years ago and

70

asked for forgiveness for the naïve and stubborn way I reacted to him because, in reality, it led me all the way to this very moment. We both danced and rejoiced together, and I brought him to the group of people I was with to introduce them to the man who planted that first seed.

The following morning, as a team, we decided that we would drive back to our church to let the congregation see how so many of us changed because of that conference and that we were hungry for more. A sweet memory still brings a smile to my face every time I think of it. As we got off the exit to get to the church, a song by Upper Room started to play, called *"Faith and Wonder."*

At the first hit of the chorus, I started to weep uncontrollably, to the point I was having a hard time driving to the church from the exit ramp. There, I ran into our church's prayer room and proceeded to weep for another 30 minutes, not knowing why or what was happening to me. It was such a sweet time with the Lord and now I can look back knowing He was giving me His heart, and I was giving Him mine.

Over the following couple of days, my life began to significantly shift. Earlier in this book, I mentioned my issues with pornography, ending my marriage, and the pain and suffering I experienced, not having the ideal relationship growing up with my parents. I had continual sin in my life up until the moments leading up to this day. The Baptism of the Holy Spirit I received that day legitimately stopped it all.

A good friend and mentor, Corey Russell put it like this, *"I fully believe in the 12-step process, but I know that there is a 1 step process and that process is called Holy Spirit."* It would be wrong for me to exclude this part simply because it would be hard to believe, but here is the fact. Since the Send, I have been completely washed free of any addiction to pornography. I have also been wiped clean from any damage that the affair and divorce could have caused over my life, and I can speak with life and love to everyone that was involved in the incident. I had a true release into what the Lord would want for them to become in their own lives, and giving Him reign in mine. It's possible for everyone to experience what I had on that Florida field. More importantly, what I experienced in my heart. With a hungry and yielded heart, the Lord can work out even the worst of issues. I know because I've been set free from them.

With a hungry and yielded heart, the Lord can work out even the worst of issues.

To explain what happened that day, I must refer back to Scripture in the book of Acts in chapter 2. The day was Pentecost, and Peter and the disciples were eagerly waiting for some "gift" Jesus mentioned to them which He said they would receive after He ascended back into Heaven. Suddenly, while all the disciples were joined together, a mighty rushing wind came into their Upper Room and the Bible states the heavens opened up over them and they began to see tongues of fire fall upon everyone in the house. Immediately, they were each filled with the Holy Spirit and they began to speak in other tongues as the Spirit gave them utterance. *Ok I know you might be reading this and just be like what? It's ok I was right there with you! Let me first explain that this is scripture.*

Recorded historical evidence of actual events that took place with actual people to which I hope can put some rest to the wandering mind. If it doesn't, I encourage you after this book to put the Bible up to the challenge, I promise this Bible has been put through the toughest of interrogations and has not failed not one accuser. A simple start would be my recommendation of watching "The Case for Christ" a movie most likely easily available to see about one man who challenged the validity of the Bible and... well you'll see the rest. So to jump back, The Bible would come to call this event in history, the Baptism of the Holy Spirit. All throughout the New Testament, we see multiple instances where supernatural miracles and divine requests were made on behalf of the apostles to see some of their situations changed by no human effort.

Questions arose within the Jewish and non-Jewish communities after people changed their views to "The Way," because of how radical and powerful the followers of Jesus were. The disciples of Jesus and early apostles that included a man named Paul from Tarsus, knew there was an indwelling power on the inside of each man and woman of God, called Holy Spirit. The evidence of tongues was the sure sign but not the only one as read earlier. Later on, in the New Testament, we begin to uncover many gifts of the Spirit and learn more on not what they are, but how to develop them.

I don't need to convince you that the Baptism of the Holy Spirit is for today, or even if it's a valid piece of our Christianity, but more so, I am explaining because I am that wondering man, who for 24 years did not follow nor study the ways of Jesus. That man was born again because of an impactful Christmas night but went on following a way of Christianity for 5 years, completely compromised in my faith. I was that man who knew about Jesus but never "knew" Him. I continued to dabble in pornography, lie, steal, maneuver my way around life, and maliciously hurt those closest to me. I had no real relationship with God because I wasn't sure I could have one. I was that man who preached the Word of God but rarely lived it and when I tried to I always knew I did it just to get attention. I'm here to not convince you, but rather explain to you that I am now fully convinced myself.

I was that man who knew about Jesus but never "knew" Him.

What happened to me at The Send was nothing short of a full-blown miracle. I had no grid for the events that took place, because even while in church, I was led to believe that there is nothing other than the Gospel and bringing people to church for today's believer in Jesus. I'm telling you on that field, the unveiling of the Spirit of God, which had been inside me since I accepted Him, ripped open and entered into every crevice of my outer man. God filled me with fire and electricity, then deposited gifts outside of tongues, and allowed me to use them even though I didn't know what they were at the time.

You may be asking what I mean by that. Well, if you turn to 1 Corinthians 14:1, the Apostle Paul eagerly asks the church to pursue the gifts of the Holy Spirit, especially to prophesy. Do you recall when I told you I was praying for people one-by-one and they wept during or after the prayer or had a shock and awe effect? Well, these are two gifts of the Spirit working hand-in-hand and I didn't even know what they were called. My prayers tapped into words of knowledge and the prophetic gifting. The Lord was downloading thoughts and prayers of people I had never met and giving me direction on how to pray for them while unlocking secrets that they left to the Lord. He was doing that to remind them of one simple truth from 1 Peter 3:12—that the Lord hears their prayers.

I proceeded to get visions that the Lord was inviting me into while praying for them. These gave them answers to desires and dreams in their heart they gave to the Lord—a prophecy as we call it. It is an unction by the Lord to give clarity to the next step.

Do you remember my Friday night at the random church? What the Lord did to me through the worship leader that night, He did to me at The Send. There's a fun quote we say at my local church when we give testimonies on what God has done in our life the past week where we end every testimony by saying *"If He can do it through me, He can do it through you."*

You still might be asking, *Derek, what does all that have to do with you getting pinned to the floor and the electricity experience?* I am here to give you the full story of my recent life with both the ups and downs. This supernatural encounter lifted my life to a much better view than I had previously while going through my trial.

I know for sure God was after one thing on that field. I had a threatening pride issue while being a Christian. When you know you're born to lead but aren't willing to humble yourself, you do the exact opposite of what Paul considers an attribute of love in 1 Corinthians 13, where he states that love is not *"puffed up."*

I had a big "I" mentality in life. I brought the team, I overcame the affair, I was getting my body healthy, me, me, me, and more of me. If the Lord needed me to do anything for Him, He wouldn't be worthy of my worship right? As a loving Father would do, He was publicly removing any sense of pride in me, while filling me back up with His heart, His power, and His mind.

We have been taught by American movies and historical leaders that power and influence must come from strength. I now follow a man who claimed to be the King of the Jews yet silenced Himself when He was questioned and accused of blasphemy.

Jesus knew that it was more important to show the world a King who didn't flex his power by his mouth but by his sacrifice. Jesus knew who He was, where He was going, and where He came from. He didn't need to prove His power because it would come in a way just a few days later louder than His voice would have been at His trial. I'm saying this beloved reader because of how truly important it is to remember one thing about the Kingdom of Heaven, there is not an **I** in it. I do not bring anything of added value to the kingdom of God, He is of all value, of all worship, and all praise.

> *Jesus knew that it was more important to show the world a King who didn't flex his power by his mouth but by his sacrifice.*

I, as a son of God, get to play a role in His beautiful story because He wants me to. You could look at what happened to me on the field and think well that is kind of weird and rude for something like that to happen to you without your consent. I gave Him my consent the moment I invited Him to live inside of me. I told him I would allow Him to do whatever he wanted to have me to Himself, and that is exactly what He did.

God, in the same instance, rebuked (called out my crap) and restored me with more of Him and completely changed the rest of my life for the better because of it. Living by and with Holy Spirit has given me insight into areas of my life I never previously addressed and has truly given me an authority unlike ever before. This authority didn't fuel some puffed-up leadership in me—it challenged me to be humble and meek and willing to let others shine more. I wanted to spend time on this topic because you might be right where I was that day. You possibly know who Jesus is, but haven't tasted that He is good, yet.

You might even have grabbed this book thinking, well, if I read this guy's story, it might give me hope in Jesus. However, you laid hands on this, I may know where you are. I get all the emotions and thoughts and feelings that surround faith and belief in Jesus.

You've read this far, and I hope with this story it's hard to deny Jesus' reality in my life, at least. I mean you sure couldn't change my mind. This book may not be leading you to change your mind right now, but I do pray that it encouraged you to simply invite Him into a discussion.

Let's say for instance your past looked similar to mine or your dating life looked similar to mine, or you might be even walking through a very similar season as I did. My story relates and so does His goodness. I am a walking testimony that when I was questioning it all, and ready to walk away, He did something only an experiential God would do. He intervened when no one could help.

I put it like this: Jesus, the one true God, is the only God that you can experience through your faith. Every other false deity is just an idea. It is pages on a book or statues to pray to. Jesus is not an idea; He is a full-blown blast of love, and peace, and power. The Bible is the only book that demands the author to be present with you while you read. He enhances every experience in your life if you allow Him.

> *Jesus, the one true God, is the only God that you can experience through your faith.*

I'm asking you to trust me, which may be crazy because you barely know me. Trust my story, trust that I have no reason to falsely accuse or puff up the truth of my story. It brings me no other pleasure than to simply know this story can help you.

Do what I did back in January of 2019, put away all you think you know, and allow God to write your story. I can tell you now as I type up these final pages to this book, I'm sitting in a coffee shop in the middle of downtown Dallas thousands of miles away from my home, currently waiting for the next step to open up, figuring out life with God. Yet, I am truly content and happy with exactly where I am.

My life is not boring. It is not hard. It is not hopeless. It's filled with excitement and joy, and full of hope, because I know my Father in heaven is good and He has good things for me. I did not earn His goodness; He is simply good. I can wait on His promises and not lose hope, nor be disheartened that they are not here yet because no matter when and how they come, they will be better than I could have ever imagined it or fulfilled it on my own.

He simply is the real deal.

Here's another kicker and this one should make you laugh. Shortly after the whole incident with my ex-wife, I started writing this very book. I remember sitting in my little nook at that apartment at my friend's house and writing like a mad man, but the book was taking such a different turn. I laugh now, but I remember thinking about all my ex-girlfriends back in high school. I was about to air out so much dirty laundry and at some point, in the year, I lost about 30 pages of the book. I was such a zealous man. I thought, Surely, the devil has blocked me from writing. I laugh now because I look back and realize it wasn't the enemy, it was God.

We are called to walk in love and if love keeps no record of wrong-doing, then my attempt to play some victim card with these women would have done the exact opposite of the original intention of this book. My intention was always simple to let you see why I now burn for Jesus and nothing else so that you can find that passion too.

I want to pray for every reader that has made it this far. This story is not any better than the one God is writing in your life right now. This story is not meant to tell you if you're going through a traumatic time in your marriage, that getting out is the solution. That was His solution for me. My heart longs to save marriages and bring them into restoration and full healing.

The enemy had a grip on my ex and me individually, way before we joined together. It inevitably led to our marriage ending, but that doesn't have to be your story. God is a redeeming God and He is so proud of those that make love work. Remember my words, love is not proven in the happy and good times, it's refined and tested in the bad and God knows how to increase our love for Him and one another during those very difficult trials we will face in our life.

He knew she and I needed to part ways because had we not parted, we probably both wouldn't be where we both are now. Even if it is not marriage, this same experience could be your relationship with your parents, or it could be your current job situation. Whatever and wherever you are right now, I can guarantee that if there is a problem in your life Jesus has the answer to it. I am encouraging you to trust Him and let Him write the story of your life.

The divorce rate between non-spiritual and Christian marriages is no different in percentages at this current rate, and also no difference in causes for why. I know my life and story added to that statistic, but I'm encouraging you that you don't have to. God wants your life to matter to your world in a way you never thought it could. He is a Father who will lead you by the hand through any trial and situation. My story wasn't hopelessness leading to divorce; it was seeing that He was making himself center in each of our lives individually because we didn't do that right. The course and direction He took each of us on were necessary for our individual calling; and ultimately, He is more interested in having each of us as His children, than losing us to the enemy's tactics. The enemy tried to win, but he didn't. It pushed us both closer to Jesus, just not together.

> *He is a Father who will lead you by the hand through any trial and situation. My story wasn't hopelessness leading to divorce; it was seeing that He was making himself center in each of our lives individually because we didn't do that right.*

I want you to know I'm praying for you right now as I speak. I'm joining in with the great Intercessor and locking arms with Him, believing for you right now. There is nothing under the sun He doesn't know about. He knows your situation. He knows how you feel and He knows it seems like there is no solution.

As I stated earlier the Bible says that our High Priest (Jesus the Intercessor) can sympathize with ALL of our weaknesses because in all points He was tempted as we are yet He was without sin. This means His words to His Father on our behalf come from a place of fully understanding where we are in our mess and more importantly our feelings and emotions. Jesus doesn't just know what scars and bruises feel like. He knows heartbreak, He knows deep loss, He knows betrayal. I am praying with Him that you may see HE is the solution because He paid to be it with His life. His desire is that He wants you to believe in the promises He has laid out for your life.

He wants you to believe that He was in the decision-making for the direction you took, even if you feel like you've veered off. He wants you to know He is always ready to bring you back into alignment with Him. I'm praying for trust to build back up in you personally, right now. It's a trust that He has, and He will always have your best interest at hand. It's a trust that He is constantly working on your behalf even if you don't see it, even if you don't feel it, He is making a way. He is confident in your ability to stay strong and rooted. Even if you don't know Him, He knows you.

If you feel this part of the book doesn't apply to you, it does. I know you have given everything else a chance for guidance, why not finally give Him that chance. He knew you before the foundations of the world and formed you in your mother's womb. He knows every detail of your life and is asking for you to trust Him with it. I'm praying that you surrender to Him today.

The plan you thought you were building, the plan with that person, business, career—His Lordship and direction is worthy to surrender to. Take it from me, a career banker who has turned his entire life around and has been enjoying life in a way he would never have had he not trusted in Jesus. I knew Him as Savior, but I didn't want Him as Lord. I'm praying that you invite both aspects of our Lord into your life. Knowing He can save you is one thing, but trusting that He will always have the best course of direction for your life, now that is a whole next level faith that I believe without a doubt, He has given all of us to have. The measure of your faith is not contingent on my story or the next person's. It's how much will YOU believe it's for you?

"Father, I release a special outpouring of your Spirit on this reader right now. I pray Lord, that you speak to them in their time of need. I pray Lord, that you show up to them in a mighty way. I pray Lord, that if they don't know who You are right now, that You will show Yourself true to them in this very moment. I also pray Lord, that if they at this moment are seeking to receive the baptism of the Holy

Spirit, that they may receive you right now, as you did in that Upper Room, wherever they are, that your Spirit comes and touches them in a mighty way. I pray for the dam in their belly to break open and for Holy Spirit to come flooding in like a mighty wave. Lord, touch your son/daughter right now—releasing the healing balm to your saint's. I pray for clarity in their hour of despair. I pray for the spirit of wisdom and revelation in the knowledge of you right now, Lord. May they have a holy confidence in the waiting, King Jesus. I thank you in advance Lord, that you will bring testimonies of your goodness from readers who encountered you while reading this book. Father, I thank you for the love that you so effortlessly give away and I bless everyone who receives this prayer in their spirit. In Jesus' precious name Amen."

I want to thank you personally for getting through this book with me. It has been quite the journey writing it and with much fear and trembling, I can smile knowing it is finished. There were seasons that I didn't think would ever come, but God. I boast in the Lord and rejoice knowing He wrote the story.

My life is far from perfection, but it's submitted to sanctification. It means I know there are areas the Lord is still working on. Yet, I am willing to allow Him to work on it because I knew the more and more, I allow for His hand to scoop out the old me, He can replace those spaces with Himself.

Madame Guyon wrote this in her book *Experiencing God through Prayer*, "the presence of His Word in your spirit is to some degree is a capacity for the reception of Himself." What the Lord revealed to me is, as I read His Word and allowed Him to read into my life. The words will jump out of the pages and start to shift my heart into alignment with what He wants for my life.

We were designed to be fully like Him and made in His image, along the years, along with the lies of the enemy, and along our own path of life, those roots of Him might have changed but can always be brought back. We renew our minds daily to bring to captivity what the world influenced us to become in order to align ourselves to what we were truly made to be in His kingdom.

These roots included things I thought I needed and things I didn't need, and things He knew I needed, and things I never knew I wanted. I told you in the beginning, this book would be raw and real, and I wasn't making it to be anything more than that. I really hope you enjoyed this book and would encourage you to consider lending this copy out or getting one as a gift.

I believe our God deserves to be praised, and what better than a story of His very own redemptive power in the life of someone who was willing to throw it all away. Know that however you received this book—whether you purchased it yourself or it was given to you, I pray you to feel His love in this book for you and believe that as you've gotten through these pages you're worthy of the same freedom He has given me.

God Bless,

Derek.

To The Reader

Hello Reader. This is Derek writing to you personally now. It's hard to know you, personally, but one day I pray I may meet you. Maybe at an event or coffee shop, you can always find me in one. I find it difficult right now to try and write to you personally because I know each of you has a different life right now. Some may not know who this Jesus person is, some may have known Him all their life. Some of you may be single, some married, and some divorced. Wherever you are as you read this, I want to break this portion of the book up to speak to each of you individually. Please don't skip over it if it doesn't apply to you. There are nuggets to gain from each portion.

Don't Know Jesus

What an opportunity to allow me, a weird Puerto Rican New Yorker, a chance to tell you about Him. This actually means so much to me that you would get not only through this book, but give the tough stuff about this book a chance. I have told you so much about Jesus already in this book and there is always more to say but rather than pump you with more, I'll simply put this section this way.

Jesus became to me something way more than a man from a book called the Bible. For so long, I dammed God more times than I could count, yet after all those terrible things, He still thought to Himself that I would be an asset to His life and that I'd be worth His death.

He thinks the same of you right now. He is so intentional about you that He somehow navigated this book into your hands and by divine grace, you find yourself all the way here 100 pages later. This wasn't all you, you didn't just choose to read this far, something about Him is intriguing you and that's ok.

You need to know how much he truly loves you right now no matter where you are. He truly died to call you His own. No matter what your past, present, or even future might look like, you need to know that Jesus decided a long time ago that you were worth Him bearing the cross. I pray that you continue to use this book and other tools to search for the man called Jesus.

I promise He doesn't fail to impress and He never misses an appointment even if we keep Him waiting. He wants you to know Him and He will recklessly search high and low to give you a chance to meet Him. Don't wait any longer!

He is inviting you into His family where you no longer will feel like an outsider or a loner but you will have the man Jesus with you the rest of your life at all times and he will never leave you. This is the God I serve and I know He is just giving you the time to choose Him today.

Walked with Jesus A Long Time

Oh, how I know this book could rattle some feathers. That's ok—this book was intended to do that. Simply, because the story itself rattled mine while I was going through it. What I can say to you friend, is that our God is vast. He is big, He is wide, and He also is deeper than the ocean. There are parts of His ocean we will never be able to search or discover. It's what makes Him God.

However, there are parts of Him that He does want us to know and He has given us an opportunity to unlock some of the mysteries if we simply put the faith forward to do so. Whatever denomination you come from I urge you to seek Jesus and ask Him, what does ALL of you look like in my life?

I know Jesus will meet you and walk you through the process of giving you His answers to your life.

Give yourself something the body of Christ has really failed to do for each other—grace. Grace is what has enabled us to even call Jesus our friend and we do not give that space to our fellow brothers and sisters and most importantly ourselves.

I need you to know you haven't missed anything. If you don't feel the kind of love, intimacy, and passion the way this book unravels, it is not too late to step into this. Get uncomfortable again.

Go lock yourself in the closet with God and talk about the things you figured were off-limits. He is your friend, your King, your Savior, but most importantly, He is your Bridegroom.

There is something special about the connection between intimate lovers and He wants that for you. Don't spare any more time and run away with Him to the mountains of His love because He wants you to experience a honeymoon with Him, whether it be your first time ever as a Christian or a trip back to the garden you once had with Him.

Single

This book is a testimony specially written and meant to be experienced by you. To simply shout loud one thing I wish someone would have told me—**wait!**

This four-letter word was once a cuss word to me, but now is the bread of life, second to Jesus for me. My heart breaks for those who look down upon this word with grief and sadness. Oh, how we have tainted and measured promises of God so close to God himself and told Him and I'd rather have the promise than the promise keeper first.

There's so much we could expand on this topic but the one thing I can leave you with was my story does not have to be yours. God wants to save the best for last that's including you. You are his very best and he only reserves the very best for His best. Do you believe that? If you do then I challenge you not to just wait so that your ministry, business, or marriage start off correctly, but most importantly finish well.

There is work being done in you personally that can only be done if the distractions are out of the way and trust me we create a lot more of them than we think of. I stress the importance of this one aspect in your life now because once it (that thing you're hoping for) comes, you will wish you had more time to prepare.

I say this with a humble and passionate heart for you, it will start off grumpy (the waiting season). Trust me, I have someone who can testify to how grumpy I was, but then as we start seeing how truly special God is and how much He satisfies all our hearts ever wanted that grumpiness dies down.

You learn the thing that kept Paul running with such effectiveness. Paul knew that the man Jesus was more attractive than anything else on this earth. We have a privilege as believers of Jesus to do something the rest of the world doesn't know how to do—"wait well." Start today beloved. It's worth the wait.

Married

My people who I also continue to dine with and love closely. My heart is filled with both excitement and distress for some of you, as I write this portion. Marriages, to believing couples have become so worn down because of the way society is changing the way we view marriage and the enemy is loving every minute of it.

Do you recall earlier when I mentioned that best friends have this beautiful story embedded within them? I said that for you. God gave me a revelation one night when I sat down and ministered to a man in leadership after discussing some marital issues that God burns to see marriages flourish because of the Kingdom friendship that lies underneath their affections and marital love.

Husbands and wives, who although have titles of a spouse, should easily run to their friendship to lean on everything that was foundational to why they got married in the first place.

We are the bride to Jesus and He is the bridegroom. On that day that He returns, riding on the Clouds in all His glory, we will not be able to turn left or right. Am I saying forget your spouse? Absolutely not.

I'm talking about getting a balance together to that place where you shared everything together. Cultivate that friendship you had when dates were fun and not just organized, and you spent hours talking on the phone, the days seemed brighter because your pursuit was to know Jesus and them.

Intimacy is not just bedroom talk. It's a heart connection to someone you have given your heart to. My plea to try this is simple. We get so bogged down with the weight of marriage that we forgot what brought us to the altar in the first place. God has an amazing way of turning even the darkest of situations into beacons of light for the world to see.

I do not desire to see what I went through to give any of you the freedom just to "get out." Fight the good fight of what—faith. Faith that you have the right spouse and that your friendship was worth all those days of smiles. Faith that by having God as the center of your marriage again, you can accomplish together what God destined your marriage to be. You both are the beacons of His love.

You ARE right now the beacon of His love. He is yielding Himself to allow your marriage to make Him shine. I encourage you as you read this to join in the celebration that heaven has for your union. They love what you have and so do I. Go after it again—full steam ahead!

Divorced

My final words… I sit amongst you now feeling like a weird minority. Like why do companies and firms have to have divorced as an option we must pick to represent our marital status? Don't we just go from married to single? Why must we claim that wretched word? *I always put single.*

There's a story I want to tell you… In Genesis, God gives Adam a task in the garden. He asks him, *"Adam, can you do me this solid I want you to name ALL the animals I have created on this earth."* (my version of the Bible) To which, Adam is absolutely down to do it. It must have been fun hearing Adam call some things out like, *"Oh yeah, that's definitely a Baboon"* I joke, but I wonder if this question ever dawned on you. How long do you think it took Adam to name them all?

Could it have been 1 month? 1 year? 10 years? Could it have been done in a day because God is just that good? Who truly knows, right? Let's go somewhere with this though.

Let's say it took him 5 years to name all the animals. What happened next? In Genesis 2:22 God lays Adam down and pulls a rib from him to create Eve—the perfect match, the one who can kindle and join him in a union. God gave him His promise of a helpmate because Adam was doing something that required assistance.

Guys, go name your animals.

86

Your life is not over; your dreams are not crushed. Stand firm, and tell the Lord that He can use you for anything and everything His heart desires. Put the oil on those bones and joints, saddle up and put your focus on Him. Go and do the things the Lord stirred your heart years ago to do that you never got around to do. Who cares about your age? Just go!

This is the only advice I can give because right now, that's exactly what I am doing. I am naming my animals and taking dominion on this earth for the Kingdom's purposes. When the Lord sees that I am about to do something that requires help, He will send my Eve. Until then, you can catch me naming my animals. I hope you will too.

Conclusion

I did not write this book with any intention to give a highlight to a "way out" for married folk or a scare factor for singles.

This book wasn't my pursuit to find happiness after an affair. It was my pursuit to find the man of Love named Jesus Christ, whom I thought I only had to understand. In his lavished ways he met me in an hour where I no longer wanted to associate with Him or his beliefs. That is His grace and mercy.

You all have read what I will call MY story, which is daily being unveiled even more. I am telling it because I have witnessed with my own eyes the redeeming love of Jesus with everyone that was involved with the story and everyone who hears it. To this day, the enemy prowls around *"like a roaring lion"* (1 Peter 5:8) to *"steal, kill, and destroy"* (John 10:10).

He destroys our singleness, steals our marriages, and kills our families because he prowls "like" a lion. The issue with our thoughts of the devil is that we can often think we know what to look for because if we see a lion, we know there's danger. My story was simply I couldn't see what that lion was because the enemy is actually more of a chameleon than a lion.

He can change his ways to not look like a lion to us so we miss the warning signs, and when I found out it was my own pursuit of what I thought Jesus was (Christian ministry) it was too late he had already devoured what I had left. **I don't blame anyone, but myself**. The Christian walk is not easy but it is the most rewarding life you could ever have.

I thought having everything I had, a wife, a great job, ministry, a great group of friends would somehow fill voids in the life I had since I was a small boy. I came to realize without actually knowing Him, the man named Jesus none of that really matters. Not making Him the priority and fulfillment of my life, and knowing and believing that He is truly the most satisfying thing I can ever have in this world. I would eventually fall short somewhere, and if not me the people I would lead out of my own brokenness.

All this didn't have to happen. I could have denied all that I heard, saw, and felt over those two months and just put my head down and sought out restoration. I'm telling you this because it still would have been a wise and honorable thing to do but I'm sure of this very reality about my journey thus far. I would have not known Jesus the way I know Him now.

I would have not had the encounter and experiences I have with Him daily because of my lack of desperate pursuit of Him prior to all this happening. God didn't send the affair or divorce so that I could get close to Him. He took what was bad and what went wrong in my marriage and saw a man that would be willing to trade his own life if he knew without a shadow of a doubt that Jesus was real.

He met my hunger and desire to know if He was true. My fear is what my life may have not looked like if I didn't listen to those words God gave me that night at that house or at that random church. The hundreds if not thousands of people that have been affected by my teachings or videos on Instagram might have never happened. I can share this with you I know I could have probably gone the rest of my life being a Christian, but I don't believe that I would have ever truly known Him. Biblically referencing Matthew 7:22-23.

Essentially, I'm informing you that you mustn't take this book and use it as justification to walk away from your marriage, to remain isolated and single, or not pursue God because we as Christians aren't any different from the rest of the world. We are broken people that found a Savior in Christ Jesus. However, in our brokenness, we have the joy to just go.

Run toward Jesus, run as fast as you can. If there is any advice I can leave it is that we can run into His arms and be free. He loves to save and He wants to save. It is His very nature to be salvation, so just get to Him before it's too late!

This book is not the Bible, and the story being written is mine alone. Your story will be better, with more focus on healing and restoration before any traumatic event even has to happen.

I believe in love and I believe in restoration. Restoration of the individual first, then the restoration of the couple. It is one of my life's callings to build back the mountain of family, for the kingdom of God. Whether that be to help one husband see his true purpose or sit with a couple and walk them through healing. I don't have many answers but I work with a guy that does (Jesus).

I pray that you don't give up until you have exercised all options including divine intervention with God. He is the Author, let Him write. You are strong and you are capable of withstanding any attack the enemy throws your way and I believe that with every fiber in my heart.

So, I urge you, don't look back—run forward. Run alone. Run together. Run with purpose, and most importantly run with Jesus. He never fails. I love you all.

P.S Stay tuned for the next book. There was a story of the events that happened within The Send that I intentionally left out which tells another beautiful story of who He is. You'll have to wait on that one till later. I love you all so much and will never cease praying for you.

Derek.

About the Author

Derek Diaz is known to many as a true rooted, free, son of God. He currently leads a small group of missionaries to help equip and develop them through his organization God Set Me Free (GSMF Worldwide. From international missions trips to local churches, you can find him speaking, counseling, and reaching the lost for Jesus. He currently lives in Dallas, Texas and is a member of Upper Room Dallas.

CPSIA information can be obtained
at www.ICGtesting.com
Printed in the USA
JSHW031921210222
23178JS00007B/202